COMPUTER SCIENCE, TECHNOLOGY AND APPLICATIONS

INFORMATION TECHNOLOGY

EFFECTIVE FEDERAL ACQUISITION AND MANAGEMENT

COMPUTER SCIENCE, TECHNOLOGY AND APPLICATIONS

Additional books in this series can be found on Nova's website under the Series tab.

Additional E-books in this series can be found on Nova's website under the E-book tab.

INTERNET POLICIES AND ISSUES

Additional books in this series can be found on Nova's website under the Series tab.

Additional E-books in this series can be found on Nova's website under the E-book tab.

COMPUTER SCIENCE, TECHNOLOGY AND APPLICATIONS

INFORMATION TECHNOLOGY

EFFECTIVE FEDERAL ACQUISITION AND MANAGEMENT

FEDELE D'ONOFRIO
EDITOR

nova publishers

New York

NOTICE TO THE READER

The Publisher has taken reasonable care in the preparation of this book, but makes no expressed or implied warranty of any kind and assumes no responsibility for any errors or omissions. No liability is assumed for incidental or consequential damages in connection with or arising out of information contained in this book. The Publisher shall not be liable for any special, consequential, or exemplary damages resulting, in whole or in part, from the readers' use of, or reliance upon, this material. Any parts of this book based on government reports are so indicated and copyright is claimed for those parts to the extent applicable to compilations of such works.

Independent verification should be sought for any data, advice or recommendations contained in this book. In addition, no responsibility is assumed by the publisher for any injury and/or damage to persons or property arising from any methods, products, instructions, ideas or otherwise contained in this publication.

This publication is designed to provide accurate and authoritative information with regard to the subject matter covered herein. It is sold with the clear understanding that the Publisher is not engaged in rendering legal or any other professional services. If legal or any other expert assistance is required, the services of a competent person should be sought. FROM A DECLARATION OF PARTICIPANTS JOINTLY ADOPTED BY A COMMITTEE OF THE AMERICAN BAR ASSOCIATION AND A COMMITTEE OF PUBLISHERS.

Additional color graphics may be available in the e-book version of this book.

Library of Congress Cataloging-in-Publication Data

ISBN: 978-1-62417-641-8

Published by Nova Science Publishers, Inc. † *New York*

CONTENTS

PREFACE

Planned federal information technology (IT) spending has now risen to at least $81 billion for fiscal year 2012. Although a variety of best practices exists to guide their successful acquisition, federal IT projects too frequently incur cost overruns and schedule slippages while contributing little to mission-related outcomes. Recognizing these problems, the Office of Management and Budget (OMB) has launched several initiatives to improve the oversight and management of IT investments. This book examines the critical factors underlying successful major acquisitions in information technology; the effective practices and federal challenges in applying agile methods in software development; and the progress made and measured results in information technology reform.

Chapter 1 – Planned federal information technology (IT) spending has now risen to at least $81 billion for fiscal year 2012. As GAO has previously reported, although a variety of best practices exists to guide their successful acquisition, federal IT projects too frequently incur cost overruns and schedule slippages while contributing little to mission-related outcomes. Recognizing these problems, the Office of Management and Budget (OMB) has launched several initiatives to improve the oversight and management of IT investments.

GAO was asked to identify (1) federal IT investments that were or are being successfully acquired and (2) the critical factors that led to the successful acquisition of these investments. To do this, GAO interviewed agency officials from selected federal departments responsible for each investment.

In commenting on a draft of GAO's report, three departments generally agreed with the report. OMB and the other departments either provided minor technical comments, or stated that they had no comments at all.

Chapter 2 – Federal agencies depend on IT to support their missions and spent at least $76 billion on IT in fiscal year 2011. However, long-standing congressional interest has contributed to the identification of numerous examples of lengthy IT projects that incurred cost overruns and schedule delays while contributing little to mission-related outcomes. To reduce the risk of such problems, the Office of Management and Budget (OMB) recommends modular software delivery consistent with an approach known as Agile, which calls for producing software in small, short increments. Recently, several agencies have applied Agile practices to their software projects.

Accordingly, GAO was asked to identify (1) effective practices in applying Agile for software development solutions and (2) federal challenges in implementing Agile development techniques. To do so, GAO identified and interviewed ten experienced users and officials from five federal projects that used Agile methods and analyzed and categorized their responses.

Chapter 3 – While investments in IT have the potential to improve lives and organizations, federal IT projects too often experience cost overruns, schedule slippages, and performance shortfalls. To address acquisition challenges, improve operational efficiencies, and deliver more value to the American taxpayer, in December 2010, OMB's Federal CIO issued a 25-point IT Reform Plan.

GAO was asked to (1) evaluate the progress OMB and key federal agencies have made on selected action items in the IT Reform Plan, (2) assess the plans for addressing action items that are behind schedule, and (3) assess the extent to which sound measures are in place to evaluate the success of the IT reform initiatives. To do so, GAO selected 10 of the 25 action items from the IT Reform Plan, focusing on the more important activities due to be completed by December 2011; analyzed agency documentation; and interviewed agency officials.

In: Information Technology
Editor: Fedele D'Onofrio

ISBN: 978-1-62417-641-8
© 2013 Nova Science Publishers, Inc.

Chapter 1

INFORMATION TECHNOLOGY: CRITICAL FACTORS UNDERLYING SUCCESSFUL MAJOR ACQUISITIONS[*]

United States Government Accountability Office

WHY GAO DID THIS STUDY

Planned federal information technology (IT) spending has now risen to at least $81 billion for fiscal year 2012. As GAO has previously reported, although a variety of best practices exists to guide their successful acquisition, federal IT projects too frequently incur cost overruns and schedule slippages while contributing little to mission-related outcomes. Recognizing these problems, the Office of Management and Budget (OMB) has launched several initiatives to improve the oversight and management of IT investments.

GAO was asked to identify (1) federal IT investments that were or are being successfully acquired and (2) the critical factors that led to the successful acquisition of these investments. To do this, GAO interviewed agency officials from selected federal departments responsible for each investment.

---

[*] This is an edited, reformatted and augmented version of the Highlights of GAO-12-7, a report to congressional committees, dated October 2011.

In commenting on a draft of GAO's report, three departments generally agreed with the report. OMB and the other departments either provided minor technical comments, or stated that they had no comments at all.

WHAT GAO FOUND

According to federal department officials, the following seven investments were successfully acquired in that they best achieved their respective cost, schedule, scope, and performance goals.

Department officials identified nine common factors that were critical to the success of three or more of the seven investments.

Investments Identified as Successful by Federal Departments

Department	Investment
Commerce	Decennial Response Integration System
Defense	Global Combat Support System-Joint, Increment 7
Energy	Manufacturing Operations Management (MOMentum) Project
Homeland Security	Western Hemisphere Travel Initiative
Transportation	Integrated Terminal Weather System
Treasury	Customer Account Data Engine 2 (CADE 2)
Veterans Affairs	Occupational Health Record-keeping System

Source: Agency data.

Common Critical Success Factors

1 Program officials were actively engaged with stakeholders.
2 Program staff had the necessary knowledge and skills.
3 Senior department and agency executives supported the programs.
4 End users and stakeholders were involved in the development of requirements.
5 End users participated in testing of system functionality prior to formal end user acceptance testing.
6 Government and contractor staff were stable and consistent.
7 Program staff prioritized requirements.
8 Program officials maintained regular communication with the prime contractor.
9 Programs received sufficient funding.

Source: GAO analysis of agency data.

Officials from all seven investments cited active engagement with program stakeholders as a critical factor to the success of those investments. Agency officials stated that stakeholders regularly attended program management office sponsored meetings; were working members of integrated project teams; and were notified of problems and concerns as soon as possible.

Implementation of these critical factors will not necessarily ensure that federal agencies will successfully acquire IT systems because many different factors contribute to successful acquisitions. Nonetheless, these critical factors support OMB's objective of improving the management of large-scale IT acquisitions across the federal government, and wide dissemination of these factors could complement OMB's efforts.

ABBREVIATIONS

CADE	Customer Account Data Engine
CBP	U.S. Customs and Border Protection
CIO	chief information officer
CMMI®	Capability Maturity Model® Integration
DHS	Department of Homeland Security
DISA	Defense Information Systems Agency
DRIS	Decennial Response Integration System
ESC	executive steering committee
FAA	Federal Aviation Administration
FEMA	Federal Emergency Management Agency
GCSS-J	Global Combat Support System-Joint
IRS	Internal Revenue Service
IT	information technology
ITIM	Information Technology Investment Management
ITWS	Integrated Terminal Weather System
LPR	License Plate Reader
MOMentum	Manufacturing Operations Management Project
NARA	National Archives and Records Administration
NNSA	National Nuclear Security Administration
NPOESS	National Polar-orbiting Operational Environmental Satellite System
OHRS	Occupational Health Record-keeping System
OMB	Office of Management and Budget

RFID	Radio Frequency Identification
SEI	Software Engineering Institute
WHTI	Western Hemisphere Travel Initiative
VA	Department of Veterans Affairs
VHA	Veterans Health Administration

October 21, 2011

The Honorable Susan M. Collins
Ranking Member
Committee on Homeland Security and Governmental Affairs
United States Senate

The Honorable Thomas R. Carper
Chairman
The Honorable Scott Brown
Ranking Member
Subcommittee on Federal Financial Management,
Government Information, Federal Services, and International Security
Committee on Homeland Security and Governmental Affairs
United States Senate

Planned federal information technology (IT) spending has now risen to at least $81 billion for fiscal year 2012. As we have previously reported, federal IT projects too frequently incur cost overruns and schedule slippages while contributing little to mission-related outcomes.[1] Given the size of these investments and the criticality of many of these systems to the health, economy, and security of the nation, it is important that federal agencies successfully acquire these systems—that is, ensure that the systems are acquired on time and within budget and that they deliver the expected benefits and functionality.

This report responds to your request that we:

1. Identify federal IT investments that were or are being successfully acquired.
2. Identify the critical factors that led to the successful acquisition of these investments.

To address our first objective, we interviewed the chief information officers (CIO) and other acquisition and procurement officials from selected departments in order to identify one mission-critical, major IT investment[2] that was, preferably, operational, and that best achieved its cost, schedule, scope, and performance goals.

To address our second objective, we interviewed officials responsible for each investment and asked them what critical factors led to the investment's success. We then categorized the critical success factors and totaled the number of times each factor was mentioned by the department and agency officials. In order to identify common critical success factors, we generalized critical success factors that were mentioned by three or more investments. We also compared the critical success factors to the Office of Management and Budget's (OMB) *25 Point Implementation Plan to Reform Federal Information Technology Management*[3] in order to determine whether those critical success factors support OMB's efforts.

We conducted our work from December 2010 through October 2011 in accordance with all sections of GAO's Quality Assurance Framework that are relevant to our objectives. The framework requires that we plan and perform the engagement to obtain sufficient and appropriate evidence to meet our stated objectives and to discuss any limitations in our work. We believe that the information and data obtained, and the analysis conducted, provide a reasonable basis for any findings and conclusions in this product. Further details of our objectives, scope, and methodology are in appendix I.

BACKGROUND

Investments in IT can enrich people's lives and improve organizational performance. For example, during the last two decades the Internet has matured from being a means for academics and scientists to communicate with each other to a national resource where citizens can interact with their government in many ways, such as by receiving services, supplying and obtaining information, asking questions, and providing comments on proposed rules.

While these investments have the potential to improve lives and organizations, federally funded IT projects can—and have—become risky, costly, unproductive mistakes. As we have described in numerous reports and testimonies,[4] although a variety of best practice documentation exists to guide their successful acquisition, federal IT projects too frequently incur cost overruns and schedule slippages while contributing little to mission-related outcomes.

IT Acquisition Best Practices Have been Identified by Industry and Government and Promoted by Legislation

IT acquisition best practices have been developed by both industry and the federal government. For example, the Software Engineering Institute[5] (SEI) has developed highly regarded and widely used guidance[6] on best practices such as requirements development and management, risk management, configuration management, validation and verification, and project monitoring and control. In the federal government, GAO's own research in IT management best practices led to the development of the Information Technology Investment Management (ITIM) Framework,[7] which describes essential and complementary IT investment management disciplines, such as oversight of system development and acquisition management, and organizes them into a set of critical processes for successful investments.

Congress has also enacted legislation that reflects IT management best practices. For example, the Clinger-Cohen Act of 1996, which was informed by GAO best practice recommendations,[8] requires federal agencies to focus more on the results they have achieved through IT investments, while concurrently improving their IT acquisition processes. Specifically, the act requires agency heads to implement a process to maximize the value of the agency's IT investments and assess, manage, and evaluate the risks of its IT acquisitions.[9]

Further, the act establishes chief information officers (CIO) to advise and assist agency heads in carrying out these responsibilities.[10] The act also requires OMB to encourage agencies to develop and use best practices in IT acquisition.[11]

Additionally, the E-Government Act of 2002 established a CIO Council, which is led by the Federal CIO, to be the principal interagency forum for improving agency practices related to the development, acquisition, and management of information resources, including sharing best practices.[12] Consistent with this mandate, the CIO Council established a Management Best Practices Committee in order to serve as a focal point for promoting IT best practices within the federal government.

Prior GAO Work Has Identified IT Acquisition Management Weaknesses, Cost Increases, and Schedule Delays on Troubled Investments

We have often reported on a range of acquisition management weaknesses facing federal IT investments—including problems relating to senior leadership, requirements management, and testing. For example, for the investments described below, we have identified acquisition weaknesses, and have reported on significant cost increases and schedule delays. Additionally, each of these investments was ultimately cancelled or significantly restructured as a result of agency reviews conducted in response to acquisition weaknesses, cost increases, and schedule delays.

- In June 2009, we reported that an executive committee for the National Polar-orbiting Operational Environmental Satellite System (NPOESS)—a program jointly managed by the Department of Commerce's National Oceanic and Atmospheric Administration, the Department of Defense, and the National Aeronautics and Space Administration—lacked the membership and leadership needed to effectively and efficiently oversee and direct the program.[13] Specifically, the Defense committee member with acquisition authority did not attend committee meetings and sometimes contradicted the committee's decisions. Further, the committee did not track its action items to closure, and many of the committee's decisions did not achieve desired outcomes. To address these issues, we recommended that the Secretary of Defense direct the key committee member to attend and participate in committee meetings. Additionally, we recommended that the heads of the agencies that participate in the committee direct the committee members to track action items to closure, and identify the desired outcomes associated with each of the committee's actions.
  Further, we reported that the launch date for an NPOESS demonstration satellite had been delayed by over 5 years and the cost estimate for the program had more than doubled—from $6.5 billion to about $15 billion.[14] In February 2010, a presidential task force decided to disband NPOESS and, instead, have the agencies undertake separate acquisitions.
- Since 2007, we have reported on a range of acquisition weaknesses facing the Department of Homeland Security's (DHS) Secure Border

Initiative Network—also known as SBI*net*. For example, in January 2010, we reported that DHS had not effectively managed key aspects of the SBI*net* testing program such as defining test plans and procedures in accordance with important elements of relevant guidance.[15] In light of these weaknesses, we made recommendations to DHS related to the content, review, and approval of test planning documentation.

In May 2010, we reported that the final acceptance of the first two SBI*net* deployments had slipped from November 2009 and March 2010 to September 2010 and November 2010, respectively, and that the cost-effectiveness of the system had not been justified.[16] We concluded that DHS had not yet demonstrated that the considerable time and money being invested to acquire and develop SBI*net* was a wise and prudent use of limited resources. The Secretary of Homeland Security ordered a departmentwide assessment of the SBI*net* program; the Secretary's decision was motivated in part by continuing delays in the development and deployment of SBI*net* capabilities and concerns that the SBI*net* system had not been adequately justified by a quantitative assessment of cost and benefits. Based on the results of the assessment, in January 2011, the DHS Secretary decided to end SBI*net* as originally conceived.

- In May 2010, we reported that after spending $127 million over 9 years on an outpatient scheduling system, the Department of Veterans Affairs (VA) has not implemented any of the planned system's capabilities and is essentially starting over.[17] After determining that the system could not be deployed, the department terminated the contract and ended the program in September 2009. We concluded that the department's efforts to successfully complete the system had been hindered by weaknesses in several key project management disciplines and a lack of effective oversight that, if not addressed, could undermine the department's second effort to replace the scheduling system. We recommended that the department take action to improve key processes, including acquisition management, requirements management, system testing, implementation of earned value management, risk management, and program oversight.

- In June 2011, we reported that end users[18] were not sufficiently involved in defining requirements for the Federal Emergency Management Agency's (FEMA) National Flood Insurance Program's insurance policy and claims management system.[19] After conducting an assessment of the program prompted by problems identified in end user testing, FEMA leadership cancelled the system because it failed to meet end user expectations. This decision forced the agency to continue to rely on an outdated system that is neither effective nor efficient. In order to avoid the root causes of this program's failure, we recommended that for future related modernization attempts, DHS should ensure that key stakeholders are adequately involved in requirements development and management.

Additionally, we have previously reported on investments in need of management attention across the federal government. For example, in April 2011, we reported[20] on the visibility into federal IT investments provided by the IT Dashboard—a publicly available website that displays detailed information on federal agencies' major IT investments, including assessments of actual performance against cost and schedule targets (referred to as ratings) for approximately 800 major federal IT investments.[21] Specifically, we reported that, as of March 2011, the Dashboard provided visibility into over 300 IT investments, totaling almost $20 billion, in need of management attention. We noted that

- 272 investments with costs totaling $17.7 billion had ratings that indicated the need for attention, and
- 39 investments with costs totaling $2.0 billion had ratings that indicated significant concerns.

OMB Has Several Initiatives under Way to Improve the Oversight and Management of IT Investments

OMB plays a key role in helping federal agencies manage their investments by working with them to better plan, justify, and determine how much they need to spend on projects and how to manage approved projects.

In June 2009, OMB established the IT Dashboard to improve the transparency into and oversight of agencies' IT investments. According to OMB officials, agency CIOs are required to update each major investment in the IT Dashboard with a rating based on the CIO's evaluation of certain aspects of the investment, such as risk management, requirements management, contractor oversight, and human capital. According to OMB, these data are intended to provide a near real-time perspective of the performance of these investments, as well as a historical perspective. Further, the public display of these data is intended to allow OMB, congressional and other oversight bodies, and the general public to hold government agencies accountable for results and progress.

In January 2010, the Federal CIO began leading TechStat sessions— reviews of selected IT investments between OMB and agency leadership—to increase accountability and transparency and improve performance. OMB has identified factors that may result in an investment being selected for a TechStat session, such as—but not limited to— evidence of (1) poor performance; (2) duplication with other systems or projects; (3) unmitigated risks; and (4) misalignment with policies and best practices.

OMB officials stated that as of June 30, 2011, 63 TechStat sessions had been held with federal agencies. According to OMB, these sessions enabled the government to improve or terminate IT investments that were experiencing performance problems. For example, in June 2010, the Federal CIO led a TechStat on the National Archives and Records Administration's (NARA) Electronic Records Archives investment that resulted in six corrective actions, including halting fiscal year 2012 development funding pending the completion of a strategic plan. Similarly, in January 2011, we reported that NARA had not been positioned to identify potential cost and schedule problems early, and had not been able to take timely actions to correct problems, delays, and cost increases on this system acquisition program.[22] Moreover, we estimated that the program would likely overrun costs by between $205 and $405 million if the agency completed the program as originally designed. We made multiple recommendations to the Archivist of the United States, including establishing a comprehensive plan for all remaining work, improving the accuracy of key performance reports, and engaging executive leadership in correcting negative performance trends.

Drawing on the visibility into federal IT investments provided by the IT Dashboard and TechStat sessions, in December 2010, OMB issued a plan to reform IT management throughout the federal government over an 18-month time frame.[23] The plan contains two high-level objectives:

- achieving operational efficiency, and
- effectively managing large-scale IT programs.[24]

To achieve these high-level objectives, the plan outlines 25 action items. According to OMB officials, they have taken several actions pursuant to this plan. For example, pursuant to Action Item Number 10—development of an

IT best practices collaboration platform—in April 2011 the CIO Council launched an IT best practices collaboration website.[25] According to OMB, this portal provides federal program managers with access to a searchable database of program management best practices in order to promote interagency collaboration and real-time problem solving related to IT programs. The portal contains links to case studies by federal agencies demonstrating the use of best practices in managing large-scale IT systems. For example, a recent case study posted by the Social Security Administration outlined efforts to develop a cadre of highly skilled, trained, and qualified program managers to promote the success of its investments.

SEVEN IT INVESTMENTS WERE REPORTED AS BEING SUCCESSFULLY ACQUIRED

According to federal department officials, the following seven investments best achieved their respective cost, schedule, scope, and performance goals.

Table 1. IT Investments Identified as Successful by Federal Departments

Dollars in millions			
Department	**Managing agency**	**Investment**	**Total estimated life-cycle costs**
Commerce	Census Bureau	Decennial Response Integration System	$1,050.0
Defense	Defense Information Systems Agency	Global Combat Support System–Joint Increment 7	$249.9
Energy	National Nuclear Security Administration	Manufacturing Operations Management Project	$41.3
Homeland Security	U.S. Customs and Border Protection	Western Hemisphere Travel Initiative	$2,000.0
Transportation	Federal Aviation Administration	Integrated Terminal Weather System	$472.5
Treasury	Internal Revenue Service	Customer Account Data Engine 2	$1,300.0 (Transition States 1 and 2)
Veterans Affairs	Veterans Health Administration	Occupational Health Record-keeping System	$34.4

Source: Agency data.

The estimated total life-cycle cost of the seven investments is about $5 billion. Six of the seven investments are currently operational. The following provides descriptions of each of the seven investments.

Commerce Decennial Response Integration System

Investment Details
Department of Commerce—U.S. Census Bureau
Number of users:
Over 10,000 call center agents and paper data capture staff between May and July 2010
Acquisition start date:
October 2005 (prime contract award)
Operations start date:
February 2010
Total estimated life-cycle costs:
$1,050.0 million through fiscal year 2011
Acquisition costs:
$505.6 million as of June 2011
Operational costs:
$536.2 million as of June 2011
Fiscal year 2012 funding request:
N/A
Source: Agency data.

The U.S. Census Bureau is the primary source of basic statistics about the population and economy of the nation and is best known for the decennial census of population and housing. The most recent decennial census was conducted in 2010. Between March and August 2010, the Census Bureau provided assistance to respondents and captured their response data via paper and telephone agent to allow sufficient time for post-capture processing, review, and tabulation. The Decennial Response Integration System (DRIS) provided a system for collecting and integrating census responses from forms and telephone interviews. Specifically, DRIS integrated the following three primary functions:

- *Paper data capture*: Processed paper census questionnaires sent by mail from respondents. The system sorted the questionnaires and captured data from them, which were turned into electronic data.
- *Telephone questionnaire assistance*: Provided respondents with assistance in understanding their questionnaire, and captured responses for forms completed over the phone. This function utilized interactive voice response as the initial contact mechanism with an option to speak with call center representatives if needed.
- *Coverage follow up*: Contacted a sample of respondents by telephone to determine if changes should be made to their household roster as reported on their initial census return with the goal of ensuring that every person in the United States is counted once and in the right place.

To help carry out the 2010 Decennial Census, the government engaged a contractor to design, build, test, deploy, implement, operate, and maintain the systems, infrastructure, staffing, procedures, and facilities needed for DRIS. The DRIS contract was divided into three primary phases. Phase 1 included the development, testing, deployment, implementation, and support of the DRIS components needed for a 2008 Census Dress Rehearsal. Phase 2 included the nationwide deployment of the DRIS components and full-scale production operations of the paper data capture, telephone questionnaire assistance, and coverage follow up functions for the 2010 Census. Phase 3 is to address post-2010 Census DRIS component disposition and data archiving. Phase 3 was to be completed in September 2011. For purposes of our report, we focused only on the first two phases of DRIS because the DRIS system was being acquired during these phases.

In October 2009, we reported that DRIS fully implemented the key practices necessary for a sound implementation of earned value management—a project management approach that, if implemented appropriately, provides objective reports of project status, produces early warning signs of impending schedule delays and cost overruns, and provides unbiased estimates of anticipated costs at completion.[26] Additionally, we reported that, as of May 2009, the DRIS contractor was experiencing a cumulative cost underrun and was ahead of schedule; however, the life-cycle cost estimate for DRIS had increased from $574 million to $946 million. This cost increase was mostly due to increases in both paper and telephone workloads. For example, the paper workload increased due to an April 2008 redesign of the 2010 Census that reverted planned automated operations to paper-based processes and required DRIS to process an additional estimated 40 million paper forms.

Defense Global Combat Support System-Joint Increment 7

The Global Combat Support System-Joint (GCSS-J) Increment 7 is a system that supports military logistics operations that provide military personnel with the supplies and information they need to accomplish their missions. GCSSJ combines data, such as the location and quantity of a particular resource, from multiple authoritative data sources (e.g., Asset Visibility, Joint Operation Planning and Execution System, and Global Decision Support System) and analyzes the data to provide information needed by logistics decision makers. The end users of the system are the logisticians at the various Combatant Commands, which are made up of representatives from multiple branches, each having a geographical or functional responsibility.[27] According to Defense Information Systems Agency (DISA) officials, the analyses generated by the system enable the commanders of the Combatant Commands to rapidly make critical decisions, and to plan, execute, and control logistics operations. Additionally, the system provides other end users with single sign-on access to the individual data sources. The diverse end user group, combined with a wide spectrum of data, provides a unified supply chain for the Army, Navy, Air Force, and Marine forces in a given area, which is to help eliminate inefficiencies and provide a more useful view into the supply chain.

DISA started GCSS-J in 1997 as a prototype. The system is being developed incrementally using Agile[28] software development— specifically, the Scrum methodology.[29] DISA is currently developing and deploying major releases for Increment 7. A total of five major releases were planned within Increment 7; Releases 7.0 and 7.1, which were implemented in March 2009 and December 2009 respectively, were the subject of our review. To date, according to DISA, Increment 7 releases have improved performance and provided new capabilities and enhancements to existing capabilities. For example, the system provides real-time information about road conditions, construction, incidents, and weather to facilitate rapid deployment of military assets.

Investment Details

Department of Defense—Defense Information Systems Agency

Number of users:
20-30 joint warfighter logistician users; 13,000 single-sign-on users

Acquisition start date:
December 2007

Operations start date:
March 2009
(deployment of initial operational capability for Increment 7)

Total estimated life-cycle costs:
$249.9 million for Increment 7 through fiscal year 2014

Acquisition costs:
$74.7 million for Increment 7 as of June 2011

Operational costs:
$61.1 million for Increment 7 as of June 2011

Fiscal year 2012 funding request:
$40.9 million for Increment 7

Source: Agency data.

Energy Manufacturing Operations Management Project

The Manufacturing Operations Management (MOMentum) Project aims to replace a suite of aging mission-essential shop floor, manufacturing control systems at the Y-12 National Security Complex[30] that support the National

Nuclear Security Administration's (NNSA) Stockpile Stewardship and Management Program. The shop floor at the Y-12 complex is responsible for the construction, restoration, and dismantling of nuclear weapon components. The core software currently used in the shop floor manufacturing control systems was deployed in the mid-1980s and will no longer be supported by the vendor on its current hardware platform beginning in 2012.

Investment Details

Department of Energy—National Nuclear Security Administration

Number of users:
350 shop floor users

Acquisition start date:
January 2009

Operations start date:
September 2010 (deployment of phase 1)

Total estimated life-cycle costs:
$41.3 million through fiscal year 2030

Acquisition costs:
$6.6 million as of June 2011

Operational costs:
$137,000 as of June 2011

Fiscal year 2012 funding request:
$6.1 million

Source: Agency data.

The MOMentum Project has two phases. Phase 1, which was the subject of our review, was implemented in September 2010, and is a deployment of the Production Planning module of SAP[31] for manufacturing planning and scheduling. Phase 2 is to include the deployment of the Manufacturing Execution module of SAP software and support the execution of production schedules on the shop floor. Phase 2 is scheduled to be completed in September 2013. The implementation of the system is expected to save $6 million annually, reduce cycle times for manufacturing, remove dependencies on obsolete technology and unsupported software, and reduce administrative errors and product deviations, among other things.

Homeland Security Western Hemisphere Travel Initiative

To facilitate inspections at the nation's 330 air, sea, and land ports of entry, the Western Hemisphere Travel Initiative (WHTI) requires all citizens of the United States and citizens of Canada, Mexico, and Bermuda traveling to the United States as nonimmigrant visitors to have a passport or other accepted document that establishes the bearer's identity and citizenship to enter the country from within the Western Hemisphere.[32] In order to implement WHTI at the land border while limiting its impact on the public, U.S. Customs and Border Protection (CBP) engaged a contractor to procure and deploy technology—including Radio Frequency Identification, License Plate Reader, and Vehicle Primary Client[33] technologies. These technologies help to provide CBP officers with law enforcement and border crossing history information for each traveler and vehicle. Initial operating capability was achieved in September 2008 when these technologies were deployed to two ports of entry. Full operating capability was achieved in June 2009 when the WHTI technology was deployed to 37 additional ports of entry. The 39 total ports of entry are high-volume land ports with 354 traffic lanes supporting 95 percent of land border traffic. After reaching full operating capability, the program's scope was expanded to include deployment of technology and processes to outbound operations, inbound pedestrian processing, and border patrol checkpoint processing.[34] For purposes of our report, we focused on the program's efforts to achieve full operating capability at 39 land ports of entry.

In October 2009, we reported that WHTI fully met 6 of the 11 key practices for implementing earned value management and partially met the remaining 5 practices.[35] Practices not fully met included, for example, a master schedule with activities that were out of sequence or lacked dependencies. Nevertheless, we reported that according to program officials, the WHTI contract was completed on time and on budget. We recommended that the department modify its earned value management policies to be consistent with best practices, implement earned value management practices that address identified weaknesses, and manage negative earned value trends.

Investment Details

Department of Homeland Security—U.S. Customs and Border Protection

Number of users:
10,000 U.S. Customs and Border Protection officers at vehicular ports of entry

Acquisition start date:
February 2007

Operations start date:
September 2008 (initial operating capability), June 2009 (full operating capability)

Total estimated life-cycle costs:
$2.0 billion through fiscal year 2019

Acquisition costs:
$343.2 million as of June 2011

Operational costs:
$255.4 million as of June 2011

Fiscal year 2012 funding request:
$80.2 million

Source: Agency data.

Additionally, in June 2010, we reported that program officials anticipated total funding shortfalls for the second phase of the program (which is outside of the scope of our review) for fiscal years 2011 through 2015.[36] Further, we reported that schedule delays for a CBP effort to upgrade local and wide area network bandwidth capacity at ports of entry could jeopardize program performance, particularly in terms of response times. Nonetheless, we noted that actual response times exceeded the expected performance levels from June 2009 to June 2010. We did not make any new recommendations at that time.

Transportation Integrated Terminal Weather System

Investment Details

Department of Transportation—Federal Aviation Administration

Number of users:
2,210 air traffic controllers and flight support personnel

Acquisition start date:
April 1995

Operations start date:
April 2003 (initial operating capability), August 2010 (full operating capability)

Total estimated life-cycle costs:
$472.5 million through fiscal year 2029

Acquisition costs:
$296.1 million as of June 2011

Operational costs:
$24.0 million as of June 2011

Fiscal year 2012 funding request:
$5.21 million

Source: Agency data.

Initially operational since April 2003, the Federal Aviation Administration's (FAA) Integrated Terminal Weather System (ITWS) provides weather information to air traffic controllers and flight support personnel. ITWS receives observation and forecast data from the National Weather Service and combines them with data from FAA terminal sensors and sensors on nearby aircraft to integrate weather hazard information for air traffic controllers, air traffic managers, and airlines. This information is presented to end users in one integrated display. According to FAA, a prototype ITWS solution was deployed to four airports beginning in 1994.

Based on those successful prototypes, FAA engaged a contractor in 1997 to design, develop, test, and deploy the ITWS system. The system was deployed to its first site in 2003; deployments to other sites continued through August 2010. According to FAA officials, one main advantage of ITWS is that it can provide a 60-minute forecast that can anticipate short-term weather changes (such as tornadoes, thunderstorms, hail, and severe icing) that could result in airplane delays or diversions to other airports, which affect the capacities at the airports. The pre-ITWS system did not have the capability to do this. According to FAA, the implementation of ITWS increases terminal airspace capacity by 25 percent in certain weather conditions and serves to maintain capacity when it would otherwise be lost.

Treasury Customer Account Data Engine 2

The Internal Revenue Service's (IRS) Business Systems Modernization program, which began in 1999, is a multibillion-dollar, high-risk, highly complex effort that involves the development and delivery of a number of modernized tax administration and internal management systems, as well as core infrastructure projects. These systems are intended to replace the agency's aging business and tax processing systems, and provide improved and expanded service to taxpayers and internal business efficiencies for IRS. One of the cornerstone projects since the inception of the Business Systems Modernization program has been the Customer Account Data Engine (CADE), which was slated to modernize taxpayer account processing through replacement of the legacy Individual Master File, a 40-year old sequential, flat-file[37] master file processing system for individual taxpayers. In August 2008, IRS began defining a new strategy—referred to as CADE 2—which would build on the progress that the current CADE processing platform had created and leverage lessons learned to date.

Investment Details

Department of the Treasury—Internal Revenue Service

Number of users:
64,000 employees

Acquisition start date:

June 2009

Operations start date:
January 2012 (estimated completion date for Transition State 1)

Total estimated life-cycle costs:
$1.3 billion for Transition States 1 and 2 though 2024

Acquisition costs:
$152.7 million as of June 2011

Operational costs:
None because the program is not yet operational

Fiscal year 2012 funding request:
$209.5 million

Source: Agency data.

IRS plans to deliver CADE 2 functionality incrementally through three phases: (1) Transition State 1, (2) Transition State 2, and (3) Target State. Transition State 1 consists of the following two projects:

- *Daily processing*: This project is to enable IRS to process and post all eligible individual taxpayer returns filed and other transactions by updating and settling individual taxpayer accounts in 24 to 48 hours with current, complete, and authoritative data, and provide employees with timely access.
- *Database implementation*: This project is to establish the CADE 2 database, a relational database[38] that will house data on individual taxpayers and their accounts; develop a capability to transfer data from the Individual Master File to the database; and provide for the access of data from the database to downstream IRS financial, customer service, and compliance systems.

In April 2011, IRS completed the Transition State 1 detailed design phase, which includes activities such as documenting the physical design of the solution. For purposes of this report, we focused only on the IRS's efforts on Transition State 1 through the completion of the detailed design phase.

In March 2011, we reported that although IRS had taken some positive steps on defining benefits, estimating costs, and managing risks for CADE 2, it did not fully identify and disclose the CADE 2 costs and benefits.[39] Specifically, we reported that

- although IRS had identified benefits for the first phase of CADE 2, it had yet to set quantitative targets for 5 of the 20 identified benefits, and had yet to finalize the benefits expected in Transition State 2 or define related quantitative targets;
- although IRS's process for developing preliminary life-cycle cost estimates was generally consistent with best practices, the agency did not perform all practices associated with credible cost estimates;
- the schedule for delivering the initial phase of CADE 2 was ambitious; and
- IRS's process for managing the risks associated with CADE 2 was generally consistent with best practices.

Our recommendations included (1) identifying all of the benefits associated with CADE 2, setting the related targets, and identifying how systems and business processes might be affected, and (2) improving the credibility of revised cost estimates.

Veterans Affairs Occupational Health Record-keeping System

Investment Details
Department of Veterans Affairs—Veterans Health Administration
Number of users: 2,000 VHA health care providers
Acquisition start date: September 2007
Operations start date: September 2009 (Increment 1)
Total estimated life-cycle costs: $34.4 million through fiscal year 2015

Acquisition costs:
$11.1 million through June 2011

Operational costs:
$1.5 million through June 2011

Fiscal year 2012 funding request:
$12.2 million

Source: Agency data.

During the development of the National Flu Plan, which was released in 2006, the White House Homeland Security Council directed VA to develop an employee health tracking and management system. According to VA officials, the need for this system became urgent due to the threat of pandemic influenza in 2007. As a result, the Veterans Health Administration (VHA), working with VA's Office of Information and Technology, developed the Occupational Health Record-keeping System (OHRS). According to VA officials, OHRS was divided into two increments. The first increment consisted of a minimum feature set which represented the functionality that would provide the agency with the largest return on investment. The first increment became operational in September 2009. The second increment was intended to add functionality to the minimum feature set and to address any remaining requirements. For purposes of our report we focused on the first increment—VA's efforts to acquire the minimum feature set. OHRS was developed using Agile software development—specifically, the Scrum methodology. OHRS serves as the electronic health record system specifically for VA employees. OHRS provides the end users (i.e., VHA employees who work in occupational health offices at VHA healthcare facilities) the ability to collect and monitor clinical data on its employees (e.g., specific immunizations and medical training) and generate reports. Additionally, a VA official stated that OHRS allows physicians to document a number of health issues related to the workforce, including training and infectious disease management. Among other things, the information in this system is used to allocate staff to appropriate patient care assignments. For example, the system can identify whether a provider has received a vaccine for a certain illness and is therefore able to treat a patient with that illness.

NINE FACTORS WERE COMMONLY IDENTIFIED AS CRITICAL TO THE SUCCESS OF MAJOR IT INVESTMENTS

Nine factors were identified as critical to the success of three or more of the seven IT investments. The factors most commonly identified include active engagement of stakeholders, program staff with the necessary knowledge and skills, and senior department and agency executive support for the program. These nine critical success factors are consistent with leading industry practices for IT acquisitions.[40] Table 2 shows the nine factors, and examples of how agencies implemented them are discussed below.

Program Officials Were Actively Engaged with Stakeholders

Officials from all seven selected investments cited active engagement with program stakeholders—individuals or groups (including, in some cases, end users) with an interest in the success of the acquisition—as a critical factor to the success of those investments. Agency officials stated that stakeholders, among other things, reviewed contractor proposals during the procurement process, regularly attended program management office sponsored meetings, were working members of integrated project teams,[41] and were notified of problems and concerns as soon as possible. For example:

- Census officials stated that the DRIS stakeholders were members of the integrated project team. Their responsibilities as members of the team included involvement in requirements development, participation in peer reviews of contractual deliverables, and review of contractor proposals.
- IRS officials told us that consistent and open communication with internal and external stakeholders has been critical to the success of CADE 2. For example, IRS officials told us that they regularly report progress made on CADE 2, as well as risk information on the program to oversight bodies, IRS executives, and IRS internal stakeholders.

In addition, officials from two investments noted that actively engaging with stakeholders created transparency and trust, and increased the support from the stakeholders. For example, NNSA officials noted that notifying

MOMentum stakeholders of potential issues as soon as they were identified helped to foster transparency and trust; this included getting stakeholders' approval to use a cost- and schedule-tracking approach that was not the agency's policy, but which ultimately saved the program money and time. Additionally, CBP officials noted that communication with the WHTI stakeholders was greatly enhanced by the use of a consistent message that described, for example, the goals of the program, deployment plans, privacy implications of the Radio Frequency Identification infrastructure, and impact of the program on select groups crossing the border, including U.S. and Canadian children and Native Americans. CBP officials stated that this standardization created a consistent, unified vision and ensured that the message stayed on course.

Table 2. Commonly Identified Critical Success Factors across Seven Successful IT Investments

	Critical success factors	Investments						
		DRIS	GCSS-J	MOMentum	WHTI	ITWS	CADE 2	OHRS
1	Program officials were actively engaged with stakeholders.	X	X	X	X	X	X	X
2	Program staff had the necessary knowledge and skills.	X		X	X	X	X	X
3	Senior department and agency executives supported the programs.	X	X		X	X	X	X
4	End users and stakeholders were involved in the development of requirements.	X	X	X		X		X
5	End users participated in testing of system functionality prior to formal end user acceptance testing.		X	X	X	X		X
6	Government and contractor staff were consistent and stable.	X	X		X	X		
7	Program staff prioritized requirements.		X	X		X		X
8	Program officials maintained regular communication with the prime contractor.	X		X	X			X
9	Programs received sufficient funding.	X			X		X	

Source: GAO analysis of agency data.

Consistent with this factor, relevant guidance[42] calls for programs to coordinate and collaborate with stakeholders in order to address their concerns and ensure that they fulfill their commitments.

Active engagement with stakeholders increases the likelihood that the program will not encounter problems resulting from unresolved stakeholder issues.

Program Staff Had the Necessary Knowledge and Skills

Officials from six of the seven selected investments indicated that the knowledge and skills of the program staff were critical to the success of the program.

This included knowledge of acquisitions and procurement processes, monitoring of contracts, large-scale organizational transformation, Agile software development concepts, and areas of program management such as earned value management and technical monitoring. For example:

- IRS officials stated that the Treasury Secretary utilized his critical position pay authority[43] to hire executives for CADE 2 who had demonstrated success in managing large-scale transformation efforts in accordance with best practices. Specifically, IRS officials stated that the CADE 2 program manager was previously responsible for the design, development, and implementation of several major global information technology solutions for a major corporation.
- CBP officials explained that a factor critical to the success of the acquisition was that almost every member of the team working on WHTI had a good understanding of acquisitions—some even held acquisition certifications—in addition to their understanding of program management. According to those officials, these skills contributed to effective program oversight of the WHTI contractors through all phases of the acquisition, not just during contract award.

Additionally, officials from three of the seven investments also cited the use of subject matter experts' knowledge in their cognizant areas as a contributing factor to their programs' successes.

For example, VA officials stated that the OHRS program relied extensively on the subject matter experts' occupational health experience—treating them as part of the development team and including them in decision making. Two investments in our sample even went one step further—by selecting the program manager from the end user organization as opposed to an individual with an IT background.

For example, NNSA officials stated that they used a project manager from the end user organization as opposed to an individual from the department's information technology office. This individual had decades of experience managing shop floor control systems.

As a result, he was well aware of how the work on the shop floor is done and focused on safely delivering the necessary functional requirements to the end user.

Leading guidance also recognizes that programs should ensure that program staffs acquire the knowledge and skills needed to perform the project.[44] Individuals who have developed the knowledge and skills needed for the programs are more likely to perform their roles effectively and efficiently.

Senior Department and Agency Executives Supported the Program

Officials from six of the seven selected investments identified support from senior department and agency executives[45] as critical to the success of their programs.

According to those officials, these senior leaders supported the success of these programs in various ways, such as by procuring funding, providing necessary information at critical times, intervening when there were difficulties working with another department, defining a vision for the program, and ensuring that end users participated in the development of the system. For example:

- The WHTI program manager told us that the former DHS Deputy Secretary reached out to another department in order to finalize a memorandum of understanding that would be used to share information on passports and passcards needed for WHTI. According to the WHTI program manager, prior to the Deputy Secretary's involvement, the other department's efforts to collaborate on this issue were not meeting the schedule requirements of the WHTI program.
  That official told us that after receiving the necessary support from the other department, CBP was able to more rapidly query that department's data.
- IRS officials explained that endorsement for CADE 2 has come from the highest levels of the organization. In particular, those officials told us that the IRS Commissioner has made CADE 2 one of his top

priorities. IRS officials told us that the Commissioner, through, for example, his keynote speech at a CADE 2 town hall meeting for IRS employees, has provided a clear and unwavering message about CADE 2.

This speech and other activities have unified IRS employees, driven change, and removed barriers that can often impede programs of this magnitude.

In our experience,[46] strong leadership support can result in benefits to a program, including providing the program manager with the resources necessary to make knowledge-based, disciplined decisions that increase the likelihood of their program's success.

End Users and Stakeholders Were Involved in the Development of Requirements

Officials from five of seven selected investments identified the involvement of stakeholders—including end users—in the requirements development process as a factor that was critical to the success of their programs. For example:

- Census officials told us that the DRIS program management office collaborated extensively with the stakeholders and the contractor to develop requirements. For example, program management office personnel, contractor staff, and the stakeholders all worked together to analyze the requirements in order to ensure they were understood, unique, and verifiable.
- VA officials told us that an OHRS end user identified a set of requirements for an occupational health system 3 years prior to the initiation of OHRS development efforts. Those officials told us that the developers worked closely with the OHRS end user representative to ensure that those requirements were still valid once the program was initiated, given the length of time since the requirements were initially identified.

Relevant industry guidance recognizes the importance of eliciting end user needs and involving stakeholders in requirements development.[47] When stakeholders and end users communicate their requirements throughout the project life cycle, the resulting system is more likely to perform as intended in the end user's environment.

End Users Participated in Testing of System Functionality Prior to Formal End User Acceptance Testing

Officials from five of the seven selected investments identified having the end users test and validate the system components prior to formal end user acceptance testing for deployment as critical to the success of their program. For example:

- DISA officials told us they used a virtual site to connect developers and end users in online testing of evolving software repeatedly during the development of GCSS-J. Using the tool, the developers were able to record the sessions, which was helpful in addressing defects identified during testing.
- CBP created a fully functional test lab facility for the WHTI program at a mock port of entry test facility constructed at an old private airport in Virginia. Using this facility, they were able to test the software that was being developed and the hardware that was being proposed. Additionally, a core end user group was established and brought to the facility multiple times a year during the acquisition to test the forthcoming technology.

Similar to this factor, leading guidance recommends testing selected products and product components throughout the program life cycle.[48] Testing of functionality by end users prior to acceptance demonstrates, earlier rather than later in the program life cycle, that the functionality will fulfill its intended use. If problems are found during this testing, programs are typically positioned to make changes that are less costly and disruptive than ones made later in the life cycle would be.

Government and Contractor Staff Were Consistent and Stable

Officials from four of the seven selected investments stated that government and contractor organizations' personnel were consistent and stable. For example:

- DISA officials indicated that the longevity of the program management office and contractor staffs has been a contributing factor to GCSS-J's success. For example, the longevity of the staff contributed to them becoming subject matter experts in their areas of responsibility.
- CBP officials explained that key program management office staff remained consistent throughout the WHTI program. In addition, according to a CBP official, the staffs genuinely liked to work with one another and were able to collaborate effectively.

This factor is consistent with relevant guidance that espouses the importance of having adequate and skilled resources.[49] In particular, having consistent and stable staff can allow teams to keep pace with their workload, make decisions, and have the necessary accountability.

Program Staff Prioritized Requirements

Officials from four of the seven selected investments cited the prioritization of requirements as enabling the efficient and effective development of system functionality. For example:

- FAA officials told us that ITWS end users presented the development team with a "wish list" of requirements that would help them significantly. Those officials told us that end users and developers prioritized those requirements by balancing importance to the end users with the maturity of the technology.
  FAA officials stated that prototypes of these new requirements were developed and evaluated by end users in the field and were ultimately implemented in the initial operating capability for ITWS.
- DISA officials explained that during development, GCSS-J end user representatives met with the GCSS-J program office and the GCSS-J developer twice a week for between a full and a half day in order to identify and prioritize requirements.
  Those officials explained that this frequent interaction was necessary because of the short development iterations (4 to 5 weeks), at the end of which useable functionality was presented to the end users for review.

The frequent prioritization ensured that the functionality most critical to the end user representative was developed, and could be deployed sooner than functionality of less importance.

Consistent with leading guidance, having prioritized requirements guides the programs in determining the system's scope and ensures that the functionality and quality requirements most critical to the end users are deployed before less-desired requirements.[50]

Program Officials Maintained Regular Communication with the Prime Contractor

Officials from four of the seven selected investments indicated that regular communication between the program management office and the prime contractor was critical to the success of the program.

This communication was proactive in that there were regularly scheduled meetings between the program management office and the prime contractor, with an expectation of full and honest disclosure of problems.

For example:

- Census officials stated that the DRIS program management office took a proactive, "no surprises" approach to communicating with the contractor.

  For example, on a monthly basis, the program management office formally documented the technical performance of the contractor based on the relevant elements of the work breakdown structure[51] and the award fee plan.[52] These reports were provided to the contractor, who in turn used the feedback to improve its technical performance.

  In addition, DRIS program managers and their contractor counterparts met weekly to discuss significant issues. DRIS officials emphasized that the expectation of open communication and trust from senior leadership fostered an environment where issues could be freely discussed with the contractor.

- CBP officials stated that during the deployment of the WHTI technology to the ports of entry, the program management office held daily conference calls with the contractor to ensure proper coordination and the rapid resolution of problems.

For example, during deployment to one port of entry it was determined that the electric system that provided power to the lanes was not adequate.

This problem was quickly identified, responsibility for resolving it was assigned, and the issue was quickly resolved.

Additionally, Census and VA officials stated that ensuring a positive, non-adversarial relationship between the prime contractor and the program management office was critical to the success of the investment. Census officials noted that both the government and the contractor staff recognized that the only way for the program to succeed was for both parties to succeed.

Consistent with this factor, leading guidance recognizes the importance of communication between program officials and the contractor organizations.[53]

Implementation of this critical success factor enables programs to ensure that requirements are understood and risks and issues are identified and addressed earlier rather than later in the process, thereby increasing the likelihood that the delivered system will meet its intended purpose and resulting in less costly and less disruptive changes and work efforts.

Programs Received Sufficient Funding

Officials from three of the seven selected investments explained that sufficient funding for the programs contributed to the success of those investments.

Officials from two of the investments attributed funding to strong congressional support; in a third case, officials cited strong leadership from senior agency and program officials as being a factor. For example:

- The WHTI program manager stated that the WHTI program received the requested funding from Congress for the 2 years leading up to the June 1, 2009, mandated implementation date.
  Additionally, that official told us that Congress provided 2-year money, that is, money that could be obligated over a period of 2 years. Officials told us that the 2year money gave the program great flexibility to accommodate the inherent complexities and expenditures incurred in a multiyear deployment, and to adapt to inevitable modifications in deployment requirements (that is, additional sites, lanes, and functionality).

- IRS officials told us that the IRS Commissioner helped the CADE 2 program obtain funding.

  For example, those officials told us that the IRS Commissioner spoke with congressional representatives frequently in order to sustain interest and support for CADE 2.

Relevant guidance recognizes the importance of sufficiently funding IT investments.[54] Investments that receive funding commensurate with their requirements are better positioned to ensure the availability of needed resources, and therefore, deliver the investment within established goals.

The nine commonly identified critical success factors are consistent with OMB's 25-point plan to improve IT management and oversight. In particular, one high-level objective of the plan—effectively managing large-scale IT programs—aims to improve areas that impact the success rates of large IT programs across the federal government.

As part of this high-level objective, the plan addresses the importance of ensuring that program management professionals have extensive experience and training, defining requirements by engaging with stakeholders, and providing senior executives with visibility into the health of their IT programs.

These principles of effective IT management are reflected in the commonly identified critical success factors.

For example, as previously mentioned, six of the seven agencies identified the knowledge and skills of program staff and five of seven agencies cited the involvement of end users and stakeholders in the development of requirements as critical to the success of their IT investments.

While our analysis of critical success factors identified by agencies resulted in nine commonly identified factors, agencies also identified additional factors as contributing to the success of their investments.

For example:

- *Agile software development*: DISA officials stated that the use of Agile software development was critical to the success of the program. Among other things, Agile enhanced the participation of the end users in the development process and provided for capabilities to be deployed in shorter periods of time.
- *Streamlined and targeted governance*: IRS officials told us that in comparison to other IRS business systems modernization projects, the governance model for CADE 2 has been streamlined.

For example, those officials stated that the CADE 2 governance structure includes an executive steering committee that, in contrast to other programs at IRS that utilize an executive steering committee, is dedicated solely to the CADE 2 program.

IRS officials told us that this gives an added measure of accountability and responsibility for the successful outcome of the program.

- *Continuous risk management*: VA officials stated that the risk management strategy that the program used was critical to its success. According to the VA officials, risks were identified at daily team meetings and mitigation strategies were developed.

  Furthermore an official explained that risk management is built in the Agile software development process by, for example, involving the end user early and often to ensure that the requirements were as thoroughly vetted as possible.

Several of these factors are also consistent with best practices, such as the critical factors relating to risk management and governance.

The full list of critical success factors and how agencies implemented them are presented in appendix II.

CONCLUDING OBSERVATIONS

Although the critical success factors identified by the seven agencies were cited as practices that contributed to the success of their acquisitions, implementation of these factors will not necessarily ensure that federal agencies will successfully acquire IT systems because many different factors contribute to successful acquisitions.

Nevertheless, the examples of how agencies implemented the critical success factors may help federal agencies address the well-documented acquisition challenges they face.

Moreover, the critical success factors in this report also support OMB's objective of improving the management of large-scale IT acquisitions across the federal government, and wide dissemination of these factors and how agencies implemented them could complement these efforts.

AGENCY COMMENTS AND OUR EVALUATION

We received written, e-mail, or verbal responses on a draft of this report from all seven departments in our review as well as OMB. These responses are summarized below.

- The Acting Secretary for the Department of Commerce provided written comments. The department stated that the report provides a good overview and assessment of governmentwide critical factors and elements that led to the successful acquisition of IT investments. The department also provided technical comments, which we incorporated as appropriate.
- An acquisition analyst from the Department of Defense CIO Acquisition Directorate, writing on behalf of the department, provided an e-mail, which stated that the department had no comments on the draft report.
- The Director of the NNSA's Office of Internal Controls, responding on behalf of the Department of Energy, provided an e-mail stating that they agreed with the report and had no further comments. They also noted that the department is committed to supporting OMB's objective of improving the management of large-scale IT acquisitions, and that wide dissemination of the factors in our report could complement OMB's efforts.
- The Director of DHS's Departmental GAO/Office of Inspector General Liaison Office provided written comments. In its comments, the department noted that it remains committed to continuing its work with OMB to improve the oversight and management of IT investments to help ensure that systems are acquired on time and within budget, and that they deliver the expected benefits and functionality. The department further stated that it will use this report to enhance and improve the factors critical to the successful acquisition of the department's investments, such as creating a structured training program to assist in obtaining certification in the program management career field, and conducting reviews to provide insight into the cost, schedule, and performance of IT investments. The department also provided technical comments, which we incorporated as appropriate.

- The Deputy Director of Audit Relations within the Department of Transportation's Office of the Secretary provided an e-mail with technical comments, which we incorporated as appropriate.
- A program analyst within the Office of the Chief Information Officer for the Department of the Treasury, writing on behalf of the department, provided an e-mail, which stated that the department had no comments on the draft report.
- The Department of Veterans Affairs Chief of Staff provided written technical comments, which we incorporated as appropriate.
- A policy analyst from OMB's Office of E-Government and Information Technology, speaking on behalf of OMB, provided verbal technical comments, which we incorporated as appropriate.

David A. Powner
Director, Information Technology Management Issues

APPENDIX I. OBJECTIVES, SCOPE, AND METHODOLOGY

Our objectives were to (1) identify federal information technology (IT) investments that were or are being successfully acquired and (2) identify the critical factors that led to the successful acquisition of these investments.

To address our first objective, we selected 10 departments with the largest planned IT budgets as reported in the Office of Management and Budget's (OMB) fiscal year 2011 Exhibit 53.

Collectively, these departments accounted for 88 percent of the federal government's requested total IT budget for fiscal year 2011. We then asked the chief information officers (CIO) and other acquisition and procurement officials from the departments to select one major, mission-critical[55] IT investment that was, preferably, operational and that best achieved its cost, schedule, scope, and performance goals. Seven departments[56]—the Departments of Defense, Commerce, Energy, Homeland Security, Transportation, the Treasury, and Veterans Affairs—identified successful IT investments.[57]

Collectively, these departments accounted for 73 percent of the planned IT spending for fiscal year 2011.

To address our second objective, we interviewed officials responsible for each investment, asking them to identify and describe the critical factors that led to their success, and to provide examples where possible.

We validated our understanding of the factors and examples collected during the interviews by providing written summaries to agency officials to ensure that their information was accurately portrayed.

Because of the open-ended nature of our discussions with officials, we conducted a content analysis of the information we received in order to identify common critical success factors.

We then totaled the number of times each factor was mentioned by department and agency officials, choosing to report on the critical success factors that were identified by three or more investments.

This resulted in our list of nine commonly identified critical success factors. We then compared these nine critical success factors to leading industry practices on IT acquisitions, such as the Software Engineering Institute's (SEI) Capability Maturity Model® Integration (CMMI®) for Acquisition, the Project Management Institute's *A Guide to the Project Management Body of Knowledge*, and GAO 's *Information Technology Investment Management: A Framework for Assessing and Improving Process Maturity*.[58]

Finally, we compared the nine commonly identified critical success factors to OMB's *25 Point Implementation Plan to Reform Federal Information Technology Management*[59] in order to determine whether those critical success factors are related to the high-level objectives found in the plan.

We conducted our work from December 2010 through October 2011 in accordance with all sections of GAO's Quality Assurance Framework that are relevant to our objectives.

The framework req uires that we plan and perform the engagement to obtain sufficient and appropriate evidence to meet our stated objectives and to discuss any limitations in our work.

We believe that the information and data obtained, and the analysis conducted, provide a reasonable basis for any findings and conclusions in this product.

APPENDIX II. CRITICAL SUCCESS FACTORS

The following seven tables provide a description of critical success factors identified by officials with each of the investments in our sample.

Table 3. Decennial Response Integration System (DRIS)—Critical Success Factors

Critical success factor	Description
Work breakdown structure-driven program organization	The DRIS work breakdown structure[a] created a set of commonly understood terms, which facilitated communication across the program. As a result, clear lines of communication and responsibility were established within and across the government and contractor program offices. Further, Census officials told us that DRIS program management documentation, including the program's schedule, requirements, and risks, aligned with the program's work breakdown structure.
Open communication with contractor through regular reviews This supports the commonly identified critical success factor: *Program officials maintained regular communication with the prime contractor.*	DRIS program managers and their contractor counterparts met weekly to discuss significant issues. Census officials emphasized that the expectation of open communication and trust from senior leadership fostered an environment where issues could be freely discussed with the contractor. The DRIS program office formally documented and communicated the technical performance of the DRIS prime contractor on a monthly basis. The contractor used this feedback to improve its performance. In addition, the contractor invited Census officials to attend working cost review meetings prior to submitting its monthly contract performance reports.[b] Census officials noted that this provided program staff with valuable insight into the contractor's performance.
Involvement of stakeholders in integrated project teams This supports the commonly identified critical success factor: *Program officials were actively engaged with stakeholders.*	DRIS stakeholders—such as Census's Population Division, which uses census data to create products like current population estimates and future population projections—were members of the DRIS integrated project teams. As part of their responsibilities as members of these teams, stakeholders were heavily involved in, for example, the development of requirements, and review of the prime contractor's deliverables.
Government and prime contractor collaboration	According to Census officials, the contractor structured its program management office to reflect the major areas of the program's work breakdown structure, and then the government structured its program management office to mirror the contractor's. Those officials told us that the mirror organizational structures and corresponding staffing positions resulted in clear lines of responsibility and communications between the two organizations. Additionally, there was a clear understanding that if the prime contractor did not succeed, the Census would in turn not succeed.

Critical success factor	Description
	Further, Census officials told us that the prime contractor adopted the same work ethic and recognized the importance of the DRIS program to the census. This partnership resulted in open communication between the prime contractor and program officials.
Government participation in contractor working meetings	The DRIS program office staff participated in the DRIS prime contractor's working meetings. For example, Census officials participated in the prime contractor's internal integrated baseline reviews.[c] Most notably, during these reviews, both the program office and an independent division of the prime contractor assessed the adequacy of the contractor's proposed performance measurement baselines. Census officials stated that this gave the DRIS program office the opportunity to hear the DRIS prime contractor's internal criticism of the proposed DRIS baselines.
Stabilized funding stream This supports the commonly identified critical success factor: *Programs received sufficient funding.*	The program consistently received the amount of funding from Congress that it requested for DRIS. These officials attributed the level of funding to strong congressional support for the program.
Consistent and stable staff with prior knowledge This supports the commonly identified critical success factor: *Government and contractor staff were consistent and stable.*	The program office consisted of officials who dedicated all of their time to the DRIS program. Additionally, those officials told us that many of the key Census officials in the DRIS program were involved in the 2000 Census. Census officials explained that the experienced staff provided expertise in the areas of paper capture technology and operations, quality assurance, call center tools and operations, and acquisitions and contract surveillance. Moreover, those officials stated that the DRIS prime contractor had experience on the 2000 Census. Census officials stated that the contractor's prior experience contributed to a stable paper capture system for DRIS and staff that were familiar with Census operations.
Early focus on managing risk	Risks were identified and mitigation strategies were prepared early in the acquisition in order to help define criteria for evaluating the proposals put forth by the potential DRIS developers. For example, the DRIS program identified information security as a significant risk to the acquisition. Consequently, program officials required potential developers to discuss information security issues during their oral presentations before the DRIS Source Selection Board.

Table 3. (Continued)

Critical success factor	Description
Contract with properly aligned incentives	The DRIS prime contract utilized an award fee[d] contract that included clear monetary incentives for the contractor to support a successful census. For example, Census officials stated that issues with the DRIS prime contractor's technical performance—one of the factors considered in the award fee structure—were quickly addressed by the prime contractor. Risk areas for the program were a factor used to determine the incentives.
Contract with clearly defined program phases	Census officials explained that because the DRIS project had three distinct phases covering a number of years, they created a contract that could evolve over time to address changes without the program being locked into one approach early on. As a result, they created a contract that could evolve to incorporate changing requirements, integrate the results of early testing, and provide a cost and schedule measurement baseline that could be updated in order to measure performance.
Cross training of business and technical staff This supports the commonly identified critical success factor: *Program staff had the necessary knowledge and skills.*	Program officials that held a technical role on the DRIS program were trained in business skills, and officials that held a business role on the program were trained in technical skills. Those officials noted that the technical training consisted of mostly on-the-job learning; the business training was a combination of classroom and on-the-job learning.
Program office and stakeholder involvement in requirements development This supports the commonly identified critical success factor: *End users and stakeholders were involved in the development of requirements.*	The DRIS program management office, stakeholders, and the contractor collaborated extensively to develop the DRIS requirements. For example, those officials told us that the program office, stakeholders, and the prime contractor analyzed the DRIS requirements to ensure that all parties had a common understanding of the requirements, that each requirement was unique, and that each requirement was verifiable.

Critical success factor	Description
Program staff trained in contracting and earned value management This supports the commonly identified critical success factor: *Program staff had the necessary knowledge and skills.*	Census officials stated that all DRIS program staff that performed surveillance on the prime contractor (i.e., oversight of the services being performed by the contractor) were trained as contracting officer's technical representatives.[e] Additionally, those officials told us that DRIS program office officials were also trained in earned value management,[f] source selection evaluations, and technical monitoring as appropriate. Many of the staff held program management certifications form the Census Bureau's project management training program.
Operational metrics drove activities	The program office and the prime contractor were unified in their efforts to satisfy the DRIS operational metrics because those metrics represented what needed to be done to ensure the success of the Census.
Incremental releases of requests for proposals	Census officials stated that they released sections of the DRIS request for proposals in draft form in order to allow for questions from prospective contractors and early feedback from DRIS stakeholders, including those involved in investment approval at the Census Bureau and the Department of Commerce. Those officials explained that the incremental releases and subsequent comments gave the program office an early opportunity to understand possible DRIS approaches. This also allowed the program to obtain the investment approvals and award the contract on schedule.
Defined forums for resolving risks and issues Focus on data quality	Each of the DRIS program's many meetings served a purpose and was held according to a defined schedule. For example, on a weekly basis, an overarching DRIS integrated project team met to discuss issues that were elevated from lower-level integrated project teams. Additionally, the purpose of each meeting was well known, and the participants were clearly defined. As such, those officials told us that DRIS team members knew where issues should be discussed and did not need to scramble to schedule meetings when an issue arose.
	Data quality was important from the very beginning of DRIS. For example, during the source selection process, the DRIS program management office provided a standard test deck of completed Census paper questionnaires to all potential developers and required them to use their prototype solution to scan this test deck in order to demonstrate the accuracy of their proposal. During the presentations, each potential developer had to discuss the data quality results from their demonstration. Additionally, an independent contractor was hired to perform independent verification and validation on the operational results of the DRIS prime contractor's paper data capture during the 2010 Census.

Table 3. (Continued)

Critical success factor	Description
Establish and update systems acquisition processes	Census-wide organizational systems acquisition processes had not been developed when DRIS was being acquired. In the absence of agency guidance, the DRIS program implemented processes from the following sources: Capability Maturity Model® Integration, best practices learned from the 2000 Census; the Seven Steps to Performance Based Contracting; relevant GAO reports; and the DRIS prime contractor's processes. The flexibility to tailor the program management processes to meet the program's specific needs contributed to the successful implementation of processes such as risk management and change management. Additionally, Census officials explained that they took steps to update and modify DRIS systems acquisition processes in order to ensure their quality. Specifically, the DRIS staff performed a "gap analysis" of the processes that they did have in place and identified processes that they needed to add. In many cases they decided to use the prime contractor's processes to fill the gaps. They also implemented a process quality assurance effort that examined one process each month to ensure that they were following the process and to solicit ideas for improving the process. In addition, on an annual basis, the DRIS program office hired an independent support contractor to review its quality assurance process in order to identify potential areas of improvement to the overall program.
Effective change control process	Census officials stated that two factors led to a change process that allowed the program to effectively control change: (1) the clear understanding of the current baseline and (2) having a change control process that was integrated with the contractor's process and which did not include unnecessary steps. Those officials added that the DRIS program performed a detailed review of each proposed change regardless of whether it was within or outside of the scope of the program.
Stopped work to replan due to contract funding	After the identification of a misalignment between Census and the prime contractor's anticipated contract funding soon after the DRIS prime contract was awarded, the program office stopped all work on the contract and worked with the prime contractor to replan the work to be performed. Census officials emphasized that it was important to stop all work so that the necessary attention and focus could be devoted to developing the replan, instead of trying to do both tasks at once.

Critical success factor	Description
Support contractor staff provided crucial skill sets This supports the commonly identified critical success factor: *Program staff had the necessary knowledge and skills.*	Census officials stated that the DRIS contractor support staff provided skill sets that were not fully possessed by the government staff, including systems architecture and information security.
Senior leadership support This supports the commonly identified critical success factor: *Senior department and agency executives supported the program.*	DRIS officials stated that involvement from Census senior leadership contributed to the success of DRIS. For example, the division chief of the Decennial Systems Contract Management Office (outside of the program management office), provided valuable information during development and testing. In addition, the Census Comptroller provided support on issues pertaining to the DRIS budget. Further, the head of the Acquisition Division helped with key pre-award and contract management challenges.

Source: GAO analysis of agency data.

[a] The work breakdown structure is a document that defines the work necessary to complete a program's objectives.

[b] The contract performance report is the primary report of cost and schedule status and provides programs with information needed for effective program control. In particular, the report provides co st and schedule variances, based on actual performance against the plan, which can be further examined to understand the causes of any differences.

[c] An integrated baseline review is held to validate that the contractor's pe rformance measurement baseline is adequate and realistically portrays all authorized work according to schedule.

[d] "Cost-plus-award-fee" contracts provide for the reimbursement of allowable costs, plus a base fee, fixed at the contract's inception (which may be zero) and an award amount that the government determines to be sufficient to motivate excellence in performance.

[e] Contracting Officer's Technical Representatives review contractor performance regularly, ensure t hat contractual milestones are met and standards are being maintained, conduct regular inspections of contractor deliverables throughout the contract period, and ensure that all contract conditions and clauses are acted upon.

[f] Earned value management is a project management approach that, if implemented appropriately, provides objective reports of project status, produces early warning signs of impending schedule delays and cost overruns, and provides unbiased estimates of anticipated costs at completion.

**Table 4. Global Combat Support System-Joint (GCSS-J) —
Critical Success Factors**

Critical success factor	Description
Stakeholder support This supports the commonly identified critical success factor: *Program officials were actively engaged with stakeholders.*	Defense Information Systems Agency (DISA) officials explained that stakeholder[a] support was critical to the successful implementation of Agile software development.[b] This support was critical because Agile introduced practices that were different from the traditional approach. For example, Agile required the continuous involvement of stakeholders in requirements development. A senior official participated in the requirements development process and also provided incentives for other stakeholders to participate as well.
Functional sponsor involvement in requirements identification and prioritization This supports the following two commonly identified critical success factors: *End users and stakeholders were involved in the development of requirements* and *Program staff prioritized requirements.*	DISA officials indicated that at the beginning of each sprint[c] the Functional Requirements Working Group, consisting of representatives from the functional sponsor, the program management office, and the contractor, met to identify which requirements were to be addressed in the release. During development the group also met twice a week for a half to full day.
Agile software development practices	DISA officials stated that the use of Agile software development was critical to the success of the program. Among other things, Agile enhanced the participation of the end users in the development process and provided for capabilities to be deployed in shorter periods of time.
Mission-focused testing This supports the commonly identified critical success factor: *Users participated in testing of system functionality prior to formal user acceptance.*	DISA officials stated that testing the system based on its ability to allow end users to perform operational tasks in support of a realistic mission was critical to the program's success. An example would be listing all of the individual steps required to load a weapon. Additionally, having the end users participate in testing at the end of each sprint helped to keep end users involved in the development process.
Integration of Agile characteristics into operational testing	DISA officials stated that integrating Agile software development characteristics into their operational testing was critical to the success of the program. Specifically, after the release went operational, the operational testers continued to collect metrics on system performance by reviewing system logs, metrics, help desk reports, remedy tickets, and problem reports to identify areas for further evaluation. For example, even though the system may have gone through the testing processes successfully, if there were an abnormally large number of end user calls a day on a certain issue during operations, the operational testers would look at their testing processes to see if there was something that they missed and how they could improve testing procedures in the future. In this way, operational testing was never "over."

Critical success factor	Description
Review board oversight	According to the DISA officials, because of the Agile software development process, the program underwent more frequent reviews that resulted in a more valid indicator of the status of the release. More frequent reviews allowed the GCSS-J stakeholders the benefit of participating frequently in the decision-making process, permitting real-time resolution of issues and problems and thus enabling the rapid release of functionality. Additionally, the officials indicated that they were able to decrease the turnaround time for certain tasks because the Milestone Decision Authority[d] had been delegated to DISA, as opposed to being at the Office of the Secretary of Defense level.
Delegation of accountability and authority	DISA officials indicated that there was empowerment to perform tasks at the lowest level. For example, the program management office was able to add pages indicating the changes that had been made to the Test and Evaluation Master Plan instead of creating a new document for each release. Additionally, according to the officials, changes to the testing process resulted in the testing period being reduced from 6 to 8 months to 2 months.
Government and contractor organizations experienced limited turnover This supports the commonly identified critical success factor: *Government and contractor staff were consistent and stable.*	A DISA official noted that the longevity of the team contributed to the success of the program. The official noted that many of the civilian staff are with the program "for life," and that the support and development contractors also have been with the program for a long time. Additionally, the longevity of the team resulted in the staff becoming subject matter experts in supporting and managing the program. For example, the Systems Design and Development Branch Chief has been with the program since 1998, and her initial duties focused on analyzing and understanding how the data the system obtained could be used. As a result, she is now a subject matter expert for issues related to the system's data.

Source: GAO analysis of agency data.

[a] A stakeholder is an individual or group with an interest in the success of an organization in delivering intended results and maintaining the viability of its products and services.

[b] Agile software development is not a set of tools or a single methodology, but a philosophy based on selected values, such as prioritizing customer satisfaction through early and continuous delivery of valuable software; delivering working software frequently, from every couple of weeks to every couple of months; and making the delivery of working software the primary measure of progress. For more information on the Agile framework, see http://www.agilealliance.org.

[c] A sprint is a block of time during which the software development team works to create a potentially usable piece of functionality. GCSS-J's sprints lasted 20 days.

[d] A Milestone Decision Authority is an acquisition official with the authority to approve a program's entry in to the next phase of the acquisition process.

Table 5. Manufacturing Operations Management Project
(MOMentum)—Critical Success Factors

Critical success factor	Description
Project manager experience with business processes This supports the commonly identified critical success factor: *Program staff had the necessary knowledge and skills.*	National Nuclear Security Administration (NNSA) officials stated that the use of a project manager from the end user organization with decades of experience on the shop floor and an awareness of how the work on the shop floor is done was critical to the success of the program. According to the officials, this gave them the ability to ensure that the requirements were fully understood prior to the implementation of the technology.
Project team empowerment	NNSA officials stated that the project team was empowered to take prudent risks, suggest new and improved approaches to meeting the required deliverables, and minimize activities that did not add value. For example, the team members were allowed to continue doing work while requirements were pending approval by the oversight board.
Developer flexibility	NNSA officials noted that the project's discrete work efforts—and associated cost, schedule, and scope commitments—were defined and managed at the highest possible level. This flexibility provided the developers with the ability to use whatever solutions and practices they thought were best to meet the needs of the end user.
Project team and contractor communication This supports the commonly identified critical success factor: *Program officials maintained regular communications with the prime contractor.*	According to NNSA officials, the potential risks of the developer's enhanced flexibility were balanced by increased communication with the project team. Specifically, the project managers from the government and developer met every week; the integrated project team[a]—which consisted of both government and developer staff—met multiple times each week; and the full MOMentum team, including government and developer staff, as well as other stakeholders, met quarterly.
Commercial off-the-shelf software compatibility	NNSA officials stated that the decision to purchase the commercial off-the-shelf software package that was most compatible with their existing system was a critical success factor. Although other commercial off-the-shelf packages might have provided superior functionality, NNSA officials determined that it would have been more difficult to integrate those other packages with their existing system.

Critical success factor	Description
Early acquisition of commercial off-the-shelf software	NNSA officials stated that the early acquisition of the commercial off-the-shelf software contributed to their success in two ways. First, because they were able to purchase the software during a time that the vendor was offering lower than normal prices, they were able to save millions of dollars on the purchase price and related licensing fees. Second, had they not acquired the software early, they would have developed their solution using a different software product, and then would have migrated that solution onto the intended software product once it was purchased. The early acquisition enabled NNSA to avoid having to migrate the solution from one product to another, thus saving time and money.
Prioritized requirements This supports the commonly identified critical success factor: *Program staff prioritized requirements.*	The program's requirements were divided into three tiers based on mission need. This allowed the program officials to prioritize the requirements and adjust the scope of the program based on the capabilities of the software. According to NNSA officials, the first tier contained mission-essential requirements, the second tier contained requirements that would only be completed if funds were available after tier one requirements were satisfied, and the third tier contained requirements that were not mission critical and would only be met if the commercial off-the-shelf software addressed them without any custom coding.
Knowledge and experience of project team This supports the commonly identified critical success factor: *Program staff had the necessary knowledge and skills.*	According to an NNSA official, the SAP[b] team at Y-12 is cited for their superior performance in SAP literature due to the complexity of the implementation and its low operating costs. Additionally, the core SAP development team at Y-12 has been working together for over a decade as the result of limited turnover.
Proactive communications with stakeholders This supports the commonly identified critical success factor: *Program officials were actively engaged with stakeholders.*	According to an NNSA official, proactive communications with stakeholders led to increased transparency. This transparency led to alternative and tailored approaches being reviewed and approved by stakeholders prior to their implementation. Additionally, the transparency contributed to a collegial, non-toxic work environment.
Tailored independent reviews based on project risk	According to an NNSA official, instead of having a large, comprehensive review of the entire program, they brought in a number of expert consultants to

Table 5. (Continued)

Critical success factor	Description
	conduct smaller, targeted reviews of the portions of the program that had the highest risks. For example, an expert in the commercial software product used for the project helped the program to validate the team's approach for modifying the software. Consequently, the program was able to limit changes to the software; this decreases the risk of a commercial product being modified to the point that it becomes a one-of-a-kind, customized solution that is no longer supported by new releases of the vendor's product, thus becoming costly to maintain.
Business owner participation in requirements development This supports the commonly identified critical success factor: *End users and stakeholders were involved in the development of requirements.*	According to an NNSA official, including the business owners in requirements development ensured that the system requirements addressed the end users' needs and that program funding would be spent on things that would contribute to meeting those needs. NNSA officials stated that obtaining feedback from the end user was facilitated by having end user representatives serve on the investment review board.
Early end user validation of functionality This supports the commonly identified critical success factor: *Users participated in testing of system functionality prior to formal user acceptance.*	MOMentum officials stated that the end users' early testing of the system's and functionality was critical to the success of the investment. Specifically, the program used conference room pilots to allow stakeholders to validate that the developers had captured all of the requirements and that the implementation of the requirements in the software was adequate. This allowed feedback to be received early in the design process where mistakes or misinterpretations could be corrected more economically than if they were discovered later during formal system testing.

Source: GAO analysis of agency data.

[a] The Office of Management and Budget defines an integrated project team as a multidisciplinary team led by a project manager responsible and accountable for planning, budgeting, procurement and life-cycle management of the investment to achieve its cost, schedule, and performance goals. Team skills include budgetary, financial, capital planning, procurement, user, program, architecture, earned value management, security, and other staff as appropriate.

[b] SAP is a company that develops commercial software under the same name. This software consists of multiple, integrated functional modules that perform a variety of business-related tasks.

**Table 6. Western Hemisphere Travel Initiative (WHTI)—
Critical Success Factors**

Critical success factor	Description
Leadership exhibited urgency and commitment This supports the commonly identified critical success factor: *Senior department and agency executives supported the programs.*	According to U.S. Customs and Border Protection (CBP) officials, senior leadership committed to implementing WHTI at land and sea ports of entry by June 1, 2009. The WHTI program manager stated that this deadline resulted in greater involvement of senior Department of Homeland Security (DHS) and CBP leadership. For example, the program manager told us that a former Deputy Secretary reached out to another agency when that agency's efforts to collaborate on an issue were not meeting the schedule requirements of the WHTI program. That official told us that after receiving the necessary support from the other department, CBP was able to more rapidly query that department's data.
Congressional support through funding This supports the commonly identified critical success factor: *Programs received sufficient funding.*	The WHTI program manager stated that the WHTI program received the requested funding from Congress for the 2 years leading up to the June 1, 2009, implementation date. Additionally, that official told us that Congress provided 2-year money, that is, money that could be obligated over a period of 2 years. Officials told us that the 2-year money gave the program great flexibility to accommodate the inherent complexities and expenditures incurred in a multiyear deployment, and to adapt to inevitable modifications in deployment requirements (that is, additional sites, lanes, and functionality).
Program office control of WHTI budget	CBP officials explained that the WHTI program budget was controlled by the WHTI program manager. Those officials stated that the WHTI program manager agreed on spending limits with the CBP offices that supported WHTI (e.g., facilities and technology) and monitored the expenditures. In contrast, CBP officials explained that funds are traditionally allocated to the CBP offices that support programs by the CBP Office of Administration. This arrangement reduces business sponsor oversight and control.
Program manager leadership	CBP officials explained that the WHTI program office was led by an experienced program manager. Those officials explained that the WHTI program manager created the necessary environment for the team to succeed. One official added that the WHTI program manager's leadership inspired the WHTI team.

Table 6. (Continued)

Critical success factor	Description
Program office knowledge This supports the commonly identified critical success factor: *Program staff had the necessary knowledge and skills.*	CBP officials explained that the WHTI program was supported by experienced staff members. CBP officials stated that almost every member of the WHTI team had a good understanding of acquisitions (demonstrated by some staff holding acquisition certifications) and program management. Further, those officials told us that the team always had two members who were knowledgeable on a particular issue— one team member was responsible for the issue and the other was a backup in the event that the primary member was not available. These skills contributed to effective program oversight of the WHTI contractors through all phases of the acquisition, not just during contract award. Moreover, one official attributed the unity of the team and the commitment to work collaboratively to the respect that each team member had for others.
Program office staff familiarity and stability This supports the commonly identified critical success factor: *Government and contractor staff were consistent and stable.*	CBP officials stated that many team members worked together on previous projects. As a result, those officials said that these team members already knew each other's role, skills, and work style, and this familiarity enabled the program office to quickly perform at a high level. Those officials added that key staff members—such as the WHTI technical leader— remained consistent throughout the WHTI program. The low turnover of WHTI program staff helped to maintain that high performance. Moreover, according to a CBP official, the staff genuinely liked to work with one another and were able to collaborate effectively.
Stakeholder involvement This supports the commonly identified critical success factor: *Program officials were actively engaged with stakeholders.*	CBP officials told us that the WHTI integrated project team was formed before the completion of planning efforts and well before the initiation of development efforts. According to CBP officials, the WHTI integrated project team was composed of numerous stakeholders such as legal support and representatives from budget/finance. CBP officials added that the team was formed prior to acquisition and development efforts, and weekly and later biweekly meetings were held with high participation rates. Those officials stated that the integrated project team was a decision-making body—not just a mechanism for the WHTI program office to communicate with stakeholders.
Consistent message when communicating	CBP officials told us that everyone in DHS and CBP— including the DHS Secretary and CBP

Critical success factor	Description
about the program	Commissioner—adhered to WHTI's consistent message and terminology when communicating with Congress, the media, and the American public. This consistent message was used to describe, for example, the goals of the program, deployment plans, privacy implications of the Radio Frequency Identification (RFID) infrastructure, and impact of the program on select groups crossing the border, including U.S. and Canadian children and Native Americans.
Daily coordination with the prime contractor during deployment This supports the commonly identified critical success factor: *Program officials maintained regular communication with the prime contractor.*	CBP officials explained that key WHTI officials participated in a 9:00 a.m. daily teleconference with the contractor while WHTI was being deployed to ensure proper coordination and the rapid resolution of problems. CBP officials explained that this daily coordination was necessary given that deployment had a significant impact on port-of-entry operations; namely, each lane was taken offline for 1 to 2 days while the infrastructure was deployed. For example, an official told us that the electric system which provided power to the lanes at a port of entry was not adequate. This official said that the issue was identified and raised during the daily morning conference, someone was assigned to begin working on the problem during that meeting, and the issue was resolved.
Prioritization of planning	CBP officials explained that their initial instinct given the aggressive implementation timeline was to focus on technical solutions, developmental efforts, and deployment. However, those officials stated that the WHTI program began with, and completed, key planning efforts which eventually secured the success of the program. Examples of these planning efforts include policy changes, regulatory requirements, and process reengineering changes.
Well-planned acquisition approach; active contract management	CBP officials explained that the program obtained extensive input from potential contractors on WHTI requirements as a result of those potential contractors' review of the draft statement of work for the WHTI design, procurement, testing, and deployment of the RFID/ License Plate Reader (LPR) infrastructure. Those officials stated that questions from the potential contractors improved the quality of the request for proposals and the resulting contract. Additionally, CBP officials explained that they utilized a fixed-price structure for the above-mentioned contract. Those officials said that this structure reduced the

Table 6. (Continued)

Critical success factor	Description
	government's risk of realizing cost overruns. Further, CBP officials stated that the contracting officer for that contract was colocated with program office officials. As a result, CBP officials explained that the contracting officer was fully aware of operational issues and requirements, provided needed guidance, and expedited contract modifications.
Testing prior to deployment This supports the commonly identified critical success factor: *Users participated in testing of system functionality prior to formal user acceptance.*	CBP officials explained that the program's testing prior to deployment was critical to the success of the WHTI program. In particular, those officials stated that the LPR and RFID design and performance were tested at a mock port-of-entry test facility constructed at an old private airport in Virginia. CBP officials said that these test lanes with RFID and LPR infrastructure were used to optimize the system so that it (1) would be able to detect multiple RFID cards in one vehicle within that lane, and (2) would not be overly sensitive as to detect RFID cards from other lanes. Additionally, those officials explained that numerous vehicle speeds, models (e.g., sedans, sports cars, SUVs, etc.), and license plate types were used to test the LPR and associated camera technologies. Further, according to CBP officials, tests were done in all weather and lighting conditions to ensure the cameras could capture acceptable images under all circumstances. Moreover, those officials told us that a group of core end users was brought to this facility to test the forthcoming technology. As a result, CBP officials explained that when many of these end users returned to their ports of entry, they became advocates for the WHTI technology.
Funding for public outreach	CBP officials stated that they believe that Congress's recognition of the significant social and cultural changes required of U.S. and Canadian citizens to successfully implement WHTI led Congress to appropriate funding for an effective communications and outreach campaign to increase awareness about new requirements for travel documents. CBP officials stated that this campaign, which relied on professional advertising media (e.g., TV, print, radio, and billboard advertising) provided by a private public relations firm, was something that normally would not be funded for a federal program, but was critical in obtaining buy-in

Critical success factor	Description
	from the local border communities and the traveling public, thus ensuring the success of the program. CBP officials explained that WHTI deployed millions of dollars in technology; however, if travelers did not obtain RFID-enabled travel documents, the technology would be underutilized. According to the WHTI program manager, because of these outreach efforts, WHTI had a compliance rate of 90 percent on the first day that WHTI documents were required to be presented at the land border.
Just-in-time operational and technical training	CBP officials told us that the end users were trained just prior to, during, and immediately after, deployment. Those officials noted that even after the lanes were accepted by CBP officials at the ports of entry, WHTI program officials stayed with the end users for 5 to 7 days to ensure that the end users were fully prepared to use the system. Those officials told us that by the time WHTI was fully implemented, over 10,000 officers had been trained in new operating procedures, application use, and familiarization with the new lane equipment and travel documents.

Source: GAO analysis of agency data.

Table 7. Integrated Terminal Weather System (ITWS)— Critical Success Factors

Critical success factor	Description
Program manager leadership	Federal Aviation Administration (FAA) officials told us that having ITWS program manager leadership that was organized, firm, and had integrity contributed to making ITWS successful. For example, those officials told us that the former program manager vigorously defended the program's budget when presenting it to senior management.
Support of senior leadership This supports the commonly identified critical success factor: *Senior department and agency executives supported the program.*	FAA officials explained that the FAA Joint Resources Council and Executive Council provided good support for the program. For example, individuals on these councils provided advice and guidance regarding acquisition procedures as well as fostering the development of leadership skills.
Consistency of program manager This supports the commonly	The program retained the same program manager for 7 years to oversee the

Table 7. (Continued)

Critical success factor	Description
identified critical success factor: *Government and contractor staff were consistent and stable.*	development and deployment of the system, which provided continuity.
Development and prioritization of requirements This supports the following two commonly identified critical success factors: *End users and stakeholders were involved in the development of requirements* and *Program staff prioritized requirements.*	FAA officials told us that ITWS end users in Orlando presented the development team with a "wish list" of requirements that would help them significantly. For example, the end users identified the need for forecasts at 10-, 20-, and 60-minute intervals. In addition, the requirements were prioritized by a team of end users and developers based on balancing their importance to the end users and the maturity of the technology.
Testing of prototypes This supports the commonly identified critical success factor: *Users participated in testing of system functionality prior to formal user acceptance.*	FAA officials stated that conceptual displays for future ITWS capabilities were presented to end users in the field. Those officials explained that these efforts helped to ensure that the end users' needs would be addressed by the operational ITWS solution.
Regular stakeholder involvement This supports the commonly identified critical success factor: *Program officials were actively engaged with stakeholders.*	The ITWS program involved stakeholders (e.g., air traffic controller labor representatives, field users, National Weather Service, Department of Defense) by inviting them to meetings every other week. Through these meetings, the former program manager explained that the program was able to obtain the stakeholder buy-in to the ITWS program.
Alignment of knowledge/expertise with tasks This supports the commonly identified critical success factor: *Program staff had the necessary knowledge and skills.*	The former ITWS program manager explained that tasks were assigned to individuals who possessed the requisite knowledge and skills. Additionally, the former program manager stated that he took steps to ensure that his staff could dedicate all of their time to the ITWS program. For example, that official told us that he utilized support contractors that were dedicated to the ITWS program.
Expectations and rewards for success	The former ITWS program manager stated that he provided the ITWS teams with a clear vision, objectives, and expectations during meetings. Additionally, that official told us that he instituted reward programs to provide incentives for the staff to be creative and get things done quickly.

Critical success factor	Description
Communication between the program management office team and the program manager	The former ITWS program manager told us that he encouraged the team to share all information with him—both successes and problems. That official told us that this environment made him aware of problems early; as a result, he was able to mitigate the impact of those problems before it became severe.
Continuous schedule management	The former ITWS program manager explained that he relied heavily on the program schedule in order to manage the program. That official added that he ensured that the official responsible for maintaining the program's schedule was present during all of the team's meetings.
Understanding of personality types This supports the commonly identified critical success factor: *Program staff had the necessary knowledge and skills.*	The former program manager for ITWS stated that the Myers-Briggs Type Indicator contributed to his ability to successfully lead the program. Specifically, that official told us that his training in the Myers-Briggs Type Indicator area helped him to understand how to communicate effectively with individuals of different types, which individuals were the best fit for a particular assignment, and who was the right person to contact to get things done on time.

Source: GAO analysis of agency data.

**Table 8. Customer Account Data Engine 2 (CADE 2)—
Critical Success Factors**

Critical success factor	Description
Senior leadership support This supports the following two commonly identified critical success factors: *Senior department and agency executives supported the programs* and *Programs received sufficient funding.*	Internal Revenue Service (IRS) officials explained that endorsement for CADE 2 has come from the highest levels of the organization. In particular, the IRS Commissioner has made the program one of his top priorities. Those officials told us that the Commissioner, through, for example, his keynote speech at a CADE 2 town hall meeting for IRS employees, has provided a clear and unwavering message about CADE 2, which has unified IRS employees, driven change, and removed barriers that can often impede programs of this magnitude. Additionally, those officials told us that the Commissioner has helped the program obtain funding for CADE 2 by speaking with Congress to sustain interest and support for the program. In addition to

Table 8. (Continued)

Critical success factor	Description
	support from the Commissioner, IRS officials stated that they have received guidance and support from the IRS Chief Technology Officer since the program's inception. For example, those officials said that CADE 2 leadership meets with the Chief Technology Officer on a monthly basis to discuss the program.
Right mix of people This supports the commonly identified critical success factor: *Program staff had the necessary knowledge and skills.*	IRS officials stated that CADE 2 leadership contains an appropriate mix of government executives that have been recruited from within and outside of IRS. Those officials explained that individuals recruited from inside IRS provide institutional knowledge and expertise on current legacy and past modernization efforts, enterprise architecture, enterprise IT operations currently in place, tax administration processes, and general administrative procedures such as hiring and budget formulation. With regard to CADE 2 executives that were recruited from external sources, IRS officials stated that the Treasury Secretary utilized his authority to authorize critical pay positions[a] for CADE 2. Officials stated that those executives have come into the IRS with demonstrated success in managing large-scale transformation efforts in accordance with best practices. For example, those officials told us that the CADE 2 program manager was previously responsible for the design, development, and implementation of several major global information technology solutions for a major corporation.
Right-sized governance model	IRS officials told us that in comparison to other IRS business system modernization projects, the governance model for CADE 2 has been streamlined. For example, those officials stated that the CADE 2 governance structure includes an executive steering committee (ESC). This committee consists of senior executives from Modernization and Information Technology Services, business partners, and the Department of the Treasury, and serves as an oversight group that ensures the program stays aligned with the IRS strategic plan and approves decisions with significant organizational or external impact. IRS officials explained that, in contrast to other programs at IRS that utilize an ESC, the CADE 2 ESC is dedicated solely to the CADE 2

Critical success factor	Description
	program. Those officials told us that this gives an added measure of accountability and responsibility for the successful outcome of the program.Additionally, IRS officials explained that because the ESC is dedicated solely to CADE 2, there is only one layer of governance below it—the Governance Board. This board consists of Associate Chief Information Officers from CADE 2 Applications Development, Enterprise Operations, Enterprise Services, and the business modernization executive from the business partner. The board ensures that objectives are met, decisions and issues are resolved in a timely manner, risks are managed appropriately, and the expenditure of resources allocated is fiscally sound. According to IRS officials, having only one layer of governance below the ESC enhances accountability and streamlines decision making and management of risks and issues. In addition to the two previously mentioned bodies, the CADE 2 program utilizes advisory councils for guidance and assistance in key areas.
Program office as system integrator	According to IRS officials, CADE 2 is the first program of its size and magnitude where the IRS has acted as the integrator and program manager over the acquisition since its inception. Consequently, those officials told us that there is a great deal of pride within IRS because employees, rather than outside contractors, are in charge of the integration and management of this substantial technology investment. Officials explained that IRS has established clear lines of authority and accountability between the CADE 2 program office (integrator), the business partners, and the delivery partners (i.e., the organizations within IRS Modernization and Information Technology Services directly responsible for the CADE 2 projects). Those officials noted that the program manager brought in a coach to drive the program office, delivery partners, and business partners to improve leadership and communication skills.
Integrated project management processes	IRS officials explained that, as the CADE 2 integrator, they have established a program framework for ensuring integration of the two projects—daily processing and database implementation—at the program level. Specifically, those officials stated that

Table 8. (Continued)

Critical success factor	Description
	they have developed a program life-cycle framework for the CADE 2 program, which includes clearly defined life-cycle phases, milestones, artifacts, and reviews. IRS officials noted that this framework enables the program office to manage the CADE 2 projects in a coordinated and integrated manner. Additionally, those officials told us that they have enhanced program management processes—such as risk management, scheduling, and requirements management—in order to account for integration at the program level. For example, IRS officials stated that they use a software tool to manage their requirements. Those officials told us that, using this tool, they now trace requirements from design through testing.
Project planning to set solid program foundation	IRS officials explained that they established four key documents in the early stages of the program: (1) a program charter, which defines the mission and goals of the CADE 2 program; (2) a solutions architecture, which describes the existing and target business processes and solutions architecture; (3) a program roadmap, which describes IRS's plan to transition from the current state to the Target State for CADE 2; and (4) a program management plan, which describes the practices and principles used to manage the program. Those officials explained that these four documents kept the team focused, and provided stability and guidance for the program.
Establishment of key milestones and decision points	IRS officials stated that during an early milestone for Transition State 1, the IRS Chief Technology Officer asked the program to clearly define the path that IRS needed to take in order to fully implement the first transition state within the planned time frame. This definition included a framework of activities which includes go/no-go decision points, deep dive reviews, independent readiness reviews, and internal confidence assessments using a confidence scoring methodology to fully inform assessments. IRS officials noted that these activities included reviews by parties external to IRS. Those officials told us that the effort to define the framework drove the program to plan more proactively

Critical success factor	Description
	for deployment at the completion of logical design review. IRS officials stated that this early deployment planning was beneficial because it provided accountability, drove contingency planning, and enhanced risk management.
Consistent and open communication This supports the commonly identified critical success factor: *Program officials were actively engaged with the stakeholders.*	IRS officials explained that they regularly report the status of CADE 2 internally to IRS employees working on the program, delivery and business partner executives, and stakeholders. For example, those officials told us that feedback forums have been established for employees and stakeholders to submit questions and obtain clarifications on the program. Further, in anticipation of the forthcoming changes associated with the January 2012 deployment of the Transition State 1 solution, IRS established a communications working group to coordinate and collaborate on CADE 2 and related IRS programs. Those officials explained that this open environment has quashed secrets and hidden agendas. Additionally, IRS officials stated that CADE 2 information is frequently shared with entities external to IRS, including oversight bodies, audit entities, and external tax advisory groups. Examples of the types of information provided include: plans, progress made, risk mitigation strategies, and information relating to the program's cost, schedule, and scope.
Use of existing contracts	IRS officials stated that because significant time is required in order to establish a new contract, IRS has utilized existing contracts to support CADE 2. Those contracts are used for activities such as program management support and technical support. Those officials noted that the use of existing contracts allowed the IRS to achieve economies of scale for large purchases. Additionally, IRS officials stated that they have been able to take advantage of the skills and expertise of contractors that have worked on the current program. For example, contract personnel with experience in creating the database that supports the current program are supporting the development of the database that will support CADE 2.

Source: GAO analysis of agency data.

[a] Critical position pay authority allows department leadership to set the rate of basic pay for a given critical position.

**Table 9. Occupational Health Record-keeping System (OHRS)—
Critical Success Factors**

Critical success factor	Description
Project team/end user representative partnership This supports the following two commonly identified critical success factors: *Program officials were actively engaged with stakeholders* and *Program staff had the necessary knowledge and skills.*	Veterans Affairs (VA) officials stated that the project was jointly owned by the end users and the project team. The end user representative was involved in daily team status meetings, various requirements development activities, and lessons-learned reviews. She was involved in decision making for things such as user interface screens and user training. As a result, the end user representative was treated as part of the project team instead of as a customer who would only be involved at the beginning or the very end of the project.
Senior leadership support This supports the commonly identified critical success factor: *Senior department and agency executives supported the programs.*	VA officials noted that senior leadership involvement was critical to the success of the acquisition. In particular, the Chief of the Office of Public Health and Environmental Hazards (located within the Veteran's Health Administration (VHA)) was committed to the success of the program and helped the program get its funding. Additionally, the Chief Consultant of the Occupational Health Strategic Healthcare Group allowed the end user representative to devote a significant amount of her time to OHRS. Furthermore, the VA Chief Information Officer and his staff participated in the early discussions regarding the need to implement OHRS.
Requirements development, prioritization, and analysis This supports the following two commonly identified critical success factors: *End users and stakeholders were involved in the development of requirements* and *Program staff prioritized requirements.*	VA officials stated that the end user representative identified a set of requirements for an occupational health system 3 years prior to the initiation of OHRS development efforts. This was critical to the success of the program because the team did not have to start requirements development from scratch. Prior to the implementation of these requirements, the end user representative and six additional subject matter experts analyzed the requirements to ensure that they were still valid given the length of time since they were initially identified. A VA official also stated that the priorities of the requirements were initially defined, then reviewed and changed throughout the project development life cycle. For example, at times it was discovered that there were requirements that needed to be implemented in conjunction with other requirements due to dependencies that were discovered later during the development.

Critical success factor	Description
Early end user testing of functionality This supports the commonly identified critical success factor: *End users participated in testing of system functionality prior to formal user acceptance.*	The end user representative tested functionality on a daily basis, approved features when they were completed at the end of each sprint, and formally approved products prior to their release. The team was able to complete quality assurance testing more quickly because the end user representative tested the product prior to the system going through more formal quality assurance testing.
Continuous risk management	VA officials stated that the risk management strategy that the program used was critical to its success. According to the VA officials, risks were identified at daily team meetings, and mitigation strategies were determined by the program management office when possible. Furthermore an official explained that risk management is built into Agile software development.[a] For example, by involving the end user early and often, VA decreased the risk that the end user would not be satisfied with the final product.
Early involvement of implementation staff	VA officials stated that bringing a member of the VA team who performs final testing and deployment onto the OHRS team early contributed to the success of the program. Specifically, those officials told us that the process of final testing and deployment was completed sooner for OHRS than some other VA systems.
Constant tracking of progress	VA officials stated that they used standardized software tools to measure and track progress of the work being done, and the associated schedule and cost. For example, the team used a software tool called "VersionOne" to track the daily progress of the development team in addressing program requirements and testing software. In addition, they used another software tool called "TeamPlay" to measure the project's major milestones, costs, and earned value on a weekly and monthly basis. The ability to manage progress contributed to the investment's success.
Project team knowledge This supports the commonly identified critical success factor: *Program staff had the necessary knowledge and skills.*	VA officials indicated that the selection of team members based on their knowledge of VHA programs, skill sets, and desire to be on an Agile team contributed to the success of the program. For example, VA officials explained that the entire team—including the end user representative—was trained in Agile software development. Those officials noted that this training was reinforced by the team's use of an Agile "coach"—an

Table 9. (Continued)

Critical success factor	Description
	individual that audited the team's Agile processes and who provided suggestions that improved the team's performance. Additionally, VA officials stated that the end user representative trained the OHRS technical staff on issues relating to occupational health and why implementation of OHRS was important.
Relationship with contractor This supports the commonly identified critical success factor: *Program officials maintained regular communication with the prime contractor.*	VA officials stated that the partnership between the government and contractor contributed to the success of the program. An official stated that the contractor and the program management office staff (in addition to the end user) met daily, which ensured they were all kept apprised of the program's status. Moreover, an official stated that the relationship between the program office and the contractor was not adversarial, which was necessary for the blended team of contractor, end user, and VA information technology staff to be successful.
Definition of performance measures	Performance measures were defined in the contract and were used by both the program management office and the contractor.
Inclusion of the contractor in planning and scheduling	According to VA officials, including the contractor in the planning and scheduling of deliverables contributed to the success of the program because it helped to ensure that the deliverables were on time.

Source: GAO analysis of agency data.

[a] Agile software development is not a set of tools or a single methodology, but a philosophy based on selected values, such as prioritizing customer satisfaction through early and continuous delivery of valuable software; delivering working software frequently, from every couple of weeks to every couple of months; and making the delivery of working software the primary measure of progress. For more information on the Agile framework, see http://www.agilealliance.org.

End Notes

[1] See, for example, GAO, *Polar-Orbiting Environmental Satellites: With Costs Increasing and Data Continuity at Risk, Improvements Needed in Tri-agency Decision Making*, GAO-09-564 (Washington, D.C.: June 17, 2009); and *Secure Border Initiative: DHS Needs to Reconsider Its Proposed Investment in Key Technology Program*, GAO-10-340 (Washington, D.C.: May 5, 2010).

[2] The Office of Management and Budget defines a major IT investment as a system or an acquisition requiring special management attention because it has significant importance to the mission or function of the agency, a component of the agency, or another organization;

is for financial management and obligates more than $500,000 annually; has significant program or policy implications; has high executive visibility; has high development, operating, or maintenance costs; is funded through other than direct appropriations; or is defined as major by the agency's capital planning and investment control process.

[3] OMB, *25 Point Implementation Plan to Reform Federal Information Technology Management* (Washington, D.C.: Dec. 9, 2010).

[4] See, for example, GAO-09-564; GAO, *Secure Border Initiative: DHS Needs to Address Testing and Performance Limitations That Place Key Technology Program at Risk*, GAO-10-158 (Washington, D.C.: Jan. 29, 2010); GAO-10-340; and *FEMA: Action Needed to Improve Administration of the National Flood Insurance Program*, GAO-11-297 (Washington, D.C.: June 9, 2011).

[5] The Software Engineering Institute is a federally funded research and development center operated by Carnegie Mellon University. Its mission is to advance software engineering and related disciplines to ensure the development and operation of systems with predictable and improved cost, schedule, and quality.

[6] See, for example, Carnegie Mellon Software Engineering Institute, Capability Maturity Model® Integration for Development (CMMI-DEV), Version 1.3 (November 2010); and Carnegie Mellon Software Engineering Institute, Capability Maturity Model® Integration for Acquisition (CMMI-ACQ), Version 1.3 (November 2010).

[7] GAO, *Executive Guide: Information Technology Investment Management, A Framework for Assessing and Improving Process Maturity*, GAO-04-394G (Washington, D.C.: March 2004).

[8] GAO, *Executive Guide: Improving Mission Performance Through Strategic Information Management and Technology: Learning from Leading Organizations*, GAO/AIMD-94-115 (Washington, D.C.: May 1994). See also, GAO, *Managing Technology: Best Practices Can Improve Performance and Produce Results*, GAO/T-AIMD-97-38 (Washington, D.C.: January 1997); and *Executive Guide: Measuring Performance and Demonstrating Results of Information Technology Investments*, GAO/AIMD-98-89 (Washington, D.C.: March 1998).

[9] 40 U.S.C. § 11312.

[10] 40 U.S.C. § 11315.

[11] 40 U.S.C. § 11302(f).

[12] 44 U.S.C. § 3603. The Federal CIO is the presidential designation for the Administrator of the OMB Office of E-Government, which was also established by the E-Government Act. 44 U.S.C. § 3602.

[13] GAO-09-564.

[14] GAO, *Polar-Orbiting Environmental Satellites: Agencies Must Act Quickly to Address Risks That Jeopardize the Continuity of Weather and Climate Data*, GAO-10-558 (Washington, D.C.: May 27, 2010).

[15] GAO-10-158.

[16] GAO-10-340.

[17] GAO, *Information Technology: Management Improvements Are Essential to VA's Second Effort to Replace Its Outpatient Scheduling System*, GAO-10-579 (Washington, D.C.: May 27, 2010).

[18] End users are the individuals or groups who will operate the system for its intended purpose when it is deployed.

[19] GAO-11-297.

[20] GAO, *Information Technology: Continued Improvements in Investment Oversight and Management Can Yield Billions in Savings*, GAO-11-511T (Washington, D.C.: Apr. 12, 2011).

[21] Available at http://www.itdashboard.gov.

[22] GAO, *Electronic Records Archive: National Archives Needs to Strengthen Its Capacity to Use Earned Value Techniques to Manage and Oversee Development*, GAO-11-86 (Washington, D.C.: Jan.13, 2011).

[23] OMB, *25 Point Implementation Plan*.

[24] The plan also outlines five subordinate goals. The high-level objective of achieving operational efficiency aligns with the goal of applying light technology and shared solutions (e.g., cloud computing, shared services across the government and consolidation of multiple organizations' data centers). The high-level objective of effectively managing large-scale IT programs aligns with the other four goals: strengthening program management; aligning the budget process with the technology cycle; streamlining governance and improving accountability; and increasing engagement with industry.

[25] Available at http://www.cio.gov/bestpractices/.

[26] GAO, *Information Technology: Agencies Need to Improve the Implementation and Use of Earned Value Techniques to Help Manage Major System Acquisitions*, GAO-10-2 (Washington, D.C.: Oct. 8, 2009).

[27] The Combatant Commands are U.S. Africa Command, U.S. Central Command, U.S. European Command, U.S. Pacific Command, U.S. Southern Command, U.S. Northern Command, U.S. Special Operations Command, U.S. Strategic Command, and U.S. Transportation Command.

[28] Agile software development is not a set of tools or a single methodology, but a philosophy based on selected values, such as prioritizing customer satisfaction through early and continuous delivery of valuable software; delivering working software frequently, from every couple of weeks to every couple of months; and making working software the primary measure of progress. For more information on Agile software development, see http://www.agilealliance.org.

[29] Scrum is one of several methodologies that are used to implement Agile software development. Scrum emphasizes developing software in increments and producing segments of functionality that are tested by, and demonstrated to, users.

[30] The Y-12 National Security Complex, located in Oak Ridge, Tennessee, is the National Nuclear Security Administration's site for conducting enriched uranium activities, producing uranium-related components for nuclear warheads and bombs, and processing nuclear fuel for the Navy.

[31] SAP is a company that develops commercial software under the same name. This software consists of multiple, integrated functional modules that perform a variety of business-related tasks.

[32] Sec. 7209, Pub. L. 108-458, Intelligence Reform and Terrorism Prevention Act of 2004 (Dec. 17, 2004), as amended; 8 U.S.C. § 1185 note. The WHTI program for land and sea ports of entry became effective on June 1, 2009, under a joint DHS and State Department final rule, 73 FR 18384, April 3, 2008. For purposes of our report, we focused only on DHS efforts to deploy WHTI at land ports of entry.

[33] According to CBP, the Vehicle Primary Client integrates vehicle and traveler information, conducts queries to law enforcement databases, and provides vehicle, traveler, query result, and crossing history information to the CBP officer.

[34] These efforts are now referred to as the Land Border Integration program.

[35] GAO-10-2.

[36] GAO, *Department of Homeland Security: Assessments of Selected Complex Acquisitions*, GAO-10-588SP (Washington, D.C.: June 30, 2010).

[37] A flat-file is a database system in which each database contains only one file, which is not linked to any other file. Flat-files are considered to be outdated technology.

[38] A relational database is a system comprised of multiple files, which can be linked to each other.

[39] GAO, *Taxpayer Account Strategy: IRS Should Finish Defining Benefits and Improve Cost Estimates*, GAO-11-168 (Washington, D.C.: Mar. 24, 2011).

[40] See, for example, SEI, CMMI® for Acquisition and GAO-04-394G.

[41] OMB defines an integrated project team as a multi-disciplinary team led by a project manager responsible and accountable for planning, budgeting, procurement, and life-cycle management of the investment to achieve its cost, schedule, and performance goals. Team skills include budgetary, financial, capital planning, procurement, user, program, architecture, earned value management, security, and other staff as appropriate.

[42] See, for example, SEI, CMMI® for Acquisition and GAO-04-394G.

[43] Critical position pay authority allows department leadership to set the rate of basic pay for a given critical position.

[44] See, for example, SEI, CMMI® for Acquisition.

[45] The term "senior department and agency executives" is used in this report to describe officials that are in the department's or agency's organizational structure, and which reside at a level above that of the programs in our sample.

[46] See, for example, GAO-04-394G and GAO, *Defense Acquisitions: Strong Leadership Is Key to Planning and Executing Stable Weapon Programs*, GAO-10-522 (Washington D.C.: May 6, 2010).

[47] See, for example, SEI, CMMI® for Acquisition.

[48] See, for example, SEI, CMMI® for Acquisition.

[49] See, for example, SEI, CMMI® for Acquisition and GAO-04-394G.

[50] See, for example, SEI, CMMI® for Acquisition.

[51] The work breakdown structure is a document that defines in detail the work necessary to complete a program's objectives.

[52] Award fees are an amount of money which a contractor may earn in whole or in part by meeting or exceeding subjective criteria stated in an award fee plan typically related to areas within quality, technical ingenuity, cost-effective management, program management, and other unquantifiable areas.

[53] See, for example, SEI, CMMI® for Acquisition.

[54] See, for example, SEI, CMMI® for Acquisition.

[55] We defined a mission-critical IT investment as one that furthered the specific mission of the department and as such would be unique to that department. For example, we did not accept an offer by a department to review the successful development and implementation of its home website, as all federal departments have home websites.

[56] The three departments that were unable to identify an IT investment that met the criteria for this engagement were the Departments of Agriculture, Health and Human Services, and Justice. The Departments of Agriculture and Health and Human Services each identified systems that they stated met our criteria; however, GAO did not agree that the systems selected were mission critical. Justice stated that it had identified an investment that met our criteria; however, it was unable to locate key documentation and evidence needed for our review.

[57] We did not independently validate the successful aspects of the investments identified for our review by the departments.

[58] SEI, *CMMI® for Acquisition*, Version 1.2 (Pittsburgh, Pa., November 2007); Project Management Institute, *A Guide to the Project Management Body of Knowledge* (PMBOK Guide), 4th ed. (Newtown Square, Pa. 2008); and GAO, *Information Technology Investment Management: A Framework for Assessing and Improving Process Maturity*, GAO-04-394G (Washington, D.C.: March 2004).

[59] OMB, *25 Point Implementation Plan to Reform Federal Information Technology Management* (Washington, D.C.: Dec. 9, 2010).

In: Information Technology
Editor: Fedele D'Onofrio

ISBN: 978-1-62417-641-8
© 2013 Nova Science Publishers, Inc.

Chapter 2

SOFTWARE DEVELOPMENT: EFFECTIVE PRACTICES AND FEDERAL CHALLENGES IN APPLYING AGILE METHODS[*]

United States Government Accountability Office

WHY GAO DID THIS STUDY

Federal agencies depend on IT to support their missions and spent at least $76 billion on IT in fiscal year 2011. However, long-standing congressional interest has contributed to the identification of numerous examples of lengthy IT projects that incurred cost overruns and schedule delays while contributing little to mission-related outcomes.

To reduce the risk of such problems, the Office of Management and Budget (OMB) recommends modular software delivery consistent with an approach known as Agile, which calls for producing software in small, short increments.

Recently, several agencies have applied Agile practices to their software projects.

---

[*] This is an edited, reformatted and augmented version of the Highlights of GAO-12-681, a report to the Subcommittee on Federal Financial Management, Government Information, Federal Services, and International Security, Committee on Homeland Security and Governmental Affairs, United States Senate, dated July 2012.

Accordingly, GAO was asked to identify (1) effective practices in applying Agile for software development solutions and (2) federal challenges in implementing Agile development techniques.

To do so, GAO identified and interviewed ten experienced users and officials from five federal projects that used Agile methods and analyzed and categorized their responses.

WHAT GAO RECOMMENDS

GAO is recommending that the Federal CIO Council, working with its chair, OMB's Deputy Director for Management, include practices such as those discussed in this report in the Council's ongoing effort to promote modular development.

After reviewing a draft of this report, OMB commented that the recommendation was better addressed to the Council than to its chair. GAO revised the recommendation to address it to the Council working with its chair.

WHAT GAO FOUND

GAO identified 32 practices and approaches as effective for applying Agile software development methods to IT projects.

The practices generally align with five key software development project management activities: strategic planning, organizational commitment and collaboration, preparation, execution, and evaluation.

Officials who have used Agile methods on federal projects generally agreed that these practices are effective.

Specifically, each practice was used and found effective by officials from at least one agency, and ten practices were used and found effective by officials from all five agencies. The ten practices are

- Start with Agile guidance and an Agile adoption strategy.
- Enhance migration to Agile concepts using Agile terms, such as user stories (used to convey requirements), and Agile examples, such as demonstrating how to write a user story.

- Continuously improve Agile adoption at both the project level and organization level.
- Seek to identify and address impediments at the organization and project levels.
- Obtain stakeholder/customer feedback frequently.
- Empower small, cross-functional teams.
- Include requirements related to security and progress monitoring in your queue of unfinished work (the backlog).
- Gain trust by demonstrating value at the end of each iteration.
- Track progress using tools and metrics.
- Track progress daily and visibly.

GAO identified 14 challenges with adapting and applying Agile in the federal environment (see table).

Finally, officials described efforts to address challenges by clarifying previously unclear guidance on using Agile.

In a related effort, the Federal Chief Information Officers (CIO) Council is developing guidance on modular development in the federal government, but it does not specifically address effective practices for Agile.

Table. Federal Challenges

Teams had difficulty collaborating closely.	Procurement practices may not support Agile projects.
Teams had difficulty transitioning to self-directed work.	Customers did not trust iterative solutions.
Staff had difficulty committing to more timely and frequent input.	Teams had difficulty managing iterative requirements.
Agencies had trouble committing staff.	Compliance reviews were difficult to execute within an iteration time frame.
Timely adoption of new tools was difficult.	Federal reporting practices do not align with Agile.
Technical environments were difficult to establish and maintain.	Traditional artifact reviews do not align with Agile.
Agile guidance was not clear.	Traditional status tracking does not align with Agile.

Source: GAO.

ABBREVIATIONS

CIO	Chief Information Officer
EVM	earned value management
IT	information technology
NASA	National Aeronautics and Space Administration
OMB	Office of Management and Budget
XP	eXtreme Programming

July 27, 2012

The Honorable Thomas R. Carper
Chairman
The Honorable Scott P. Brown
Ranking Member
Subcommittee on Federal Financial Management, Government
Information, Federal Services, and International Security
Committee on Homeland Security and Governmental Affairs
United States Senate

Information systems are integral to many aspects of federal government operations. To support agency missions, the federal government spent at least $76 billion in fiscal year 2011 on information technology (IT). However, as we have previously reported, prior IT expenditures too often have produced disappointing results, including multimillion dollar cost overruns and schedule delays measured in years, with questionable mission-related achievements.[1] Congress has expressed long-standing interest in monitoring and improving federal IT investments, which have often been developed in long, sequential phases. Recently, several agencies have tried an alternate approach known as Agile, which calls for producing software in small, short increments.

Shorter, more incremental approaches to IT development have been identified as having the potential to improve the way in which the federal government develops and implements IT. For example, the Office of Management and Budget (OMB) recently issued guidance that advocates the use of shorter delivery time frames, an approach consistent with Agile.[2] As federal interest in Agile grows, it is helpful to know how experienced users effectively follow this approach and what challenges it presents in the federal environment.

Accordingly, the objectives of our review were to identify (1) effective practices in applying Agile for software development solutions and (2) federal challenges in implementing Agile development techniques.

To identify effective practices in applying Agile for software development solutions, we interviewed a nongeneralizable sample of experienced Agile users (see app. III).[3] We identified those users from publications, forums, and recommendations from federal and private officials knowledgeable about Agile. To ensure a broad range of experiences, we chose individuals from private, public, and non-profit backgrounds. We asked them individually to describe what they have found to be effective practices in applying Agile methods. We compiled the practices and asked the users to rate them for effectiveness. We then asked officials from a nongeneralizable sample of five federal software development projects that had used Agile methods for their views on the effectiveness of the practices. The projects were selected to reflect a range of agencies, system descriptions, and cost. The five federal agencies supporting these projects were the Departments of Commerce, Defense, and Veterans Affairs, the Internal Revenue Service, and the National Aeronautics and Space Administration (see app. IV for additional information on the projects and responsible officials).

To identify federal challenges in implementing Agile development techniques, we asked the officials from the five projects to identify challenges applying Agile in their agency and efforts they had taken to address these challenges. We analyzed their responses and categorized them by topic.

We conducted our work from October 2011 through July 2012 in accordance with all sections of GAO's Quality Assurance Framework that were relevant to our objectives. The framework requires that we plan and perform the engagement to obtain sufficient and appropriate evidence to meet our stated objectives and to discuss any limitations in our work. We believe that the information obtained provides a reasonable basis for our findings and conclusions based on our audit objectives. Further details of our objectives, scope, and methodology are in appendix I.

BACKGROUND

While federal IT investments can improve operational performance and increase public interaction with government, too often they have become risky, costly, and unproductive mistakes. Congress has expressed interest in monitoring and improving IT investments through hearings and other reviews over the past two decades. In response, we have testified and reported on lengthy federal IT projects that too frequently incur cost overruns and schedule slippages while contributing little to mission-related outcomes.[4] Similarly, in 2010, OMB expressed concern about expansive federal IT projects that have taken years and have failed at alarming rates. OMB also noted that many projects follow "grand designs" to deliver functionality in years, rather than breaking projects into more manageable chunks and delivering functionality every few quarters.

One approach to reducing the risks from broadly scoped, multiyear projects is the use of shorter software delivery times, a technique advocated by OMB in recent guidance documents. Specifically, OMB's June 2010 memo on IT financial system reforms and the December 2010 IT management reform plan[5] encourage modular development with usable functionality delivered in 90 to 120 days. In addition, the Federal Chief Information Officers (CIO) Council, chaired by OMB's Deputy Director for Management, encourages the sharing and adoption of efficient IT development practices, such as those in OMB's IT guidance. The Council is comprised of CIOs and Deputy CIOs of 28 agencies. It is the principal interagency forum for improving agency practices related to the design, acquisition, development, modernization, use, sharing, and performance of federal information resources.

Agile software development supports the practice of shorter software delivery. Specifically, Agile calls for the delivery of software in small, short increments rather than in the typically long, sequential phases of a traditional waterfall approach. More a philosophy than a methodology, Agile emphasizes this early and continuous software delivery, as well as using collaborative teams, and measuring progress with working software. The Agile approach was first articulated in a 2001 document called the Agile Manifesto, which is still used today. The manifesto has four values: (1) individuals and interactions over processes and tools, (2) working software over comprehensive documentation, (3) customer collaboration over contract negotiation, and (4) responding to change over following a plan.[6] Appendix II provides additional information on the Agile Manifesto and its related principles.

Agile and Waterfall Approaches Differ

The Agile approach differs in several ways from traditional waterfall software development,[7] which produces a full software product at the end of a sequence of phases. For example, the two approaches differ in (1) the timing and scope of software development and delivery, (2) the timing and scope of project planning, (3) project status evaluation, and (4) collaboration.

- **Timing and scope of software development and delivery.** In an Agile project, working software is produced in iterations of typically one to eight weeks in duration, each of which provides a segment of functionality. To allow completion within the short time frame, each iteration is relatively small in scope. For example, an iteration could encompass a single function within a multistep process for documenting and reporting insurance claims, such as a data entry screen or a link to a database. Iterations combine into releases, with the number of iterations dependent on the scope of the multistep process. To meet the goal of delivering working software, teams perform each of the steps of traditional software development for each iteration. Specifically, for each iteration, the teams identify requirements, design, and develop software to meet those requirements, and test the resulting software to determine if it meets the stated requirements. In contrast, waterfall development proceeds in sequential phases of no consistent, fixed duration to produce a complete system, such as one that addresses a comprehensive set of steps to manage insurance claims. Such full system development efforts can take several years. Waterfall phases typically address a single step in the development cycle. For example, in one phase, customer requirements for the complete product are documented, reviewed, and handed to technical staff. One or more phases follow, in which the technical staff develop software to meet those requirements. In the final phase, the software is tested and reviewed for compliance with the identified requirements.
- **Timing and scope of project planning.** In Agile, initial planning regarding cost, scope, and timing is conducted at a high level. However, these initial plans are supplemented by more specific plans for each iteration and the overall plans can be revised to reflect experience from completed iterations. For example, desired project outcomes might initially be captured in a broad vision statement that provides the basis for developing specific outcomes for an iteration. Once an iteration has been completed, the overall plans can be revised to reflect the completed work and any knowledge gained during the iteration. For example, initial cost and schedule estimates can be revised to reflect the actual cost and timing of the completed work. In

contrast, in traditional waterfall project management, this analysis is documented in detail at the beginning of the project for the entire scope of work. For example, significant effort may be devoted to documenting strategies, project plans, cost and schedule estimates, and requirements for a full system.

- **Project status evaluation.** In Agile, project status is primarily evaluated based on software demonstrations. For example, iterations typically end with a demonstration for customers and stakeholders of the working software produced during that iteration. The demonstration can reveal requirements that were not fully addressed during the iteration or the discovery of new requirements. These incomplete or newly-identified requirements are queued for possible inclusion in later iterations. In contrast, in traditional project management, progress is assessed based on a review of data and documents at predetermined milestones and checkpoints. Milestones and checkpoints can occur at the end of a phase, such as the end of requirements definition, or at scheduled intervals, such as monthly. The reviews typically include status reports on work done to date and a comparison of the project's actual cost and schedule to baseline projections. Federal IT evaluation guidance, such as our IT Investment Management guidance[8] and OMB IT reporting requirements[9] specify evaluations at key milestones, and annually, which more closely align with traditional development methods. For example, for major projects, OMB requires a monthly comparison of actual and planned cost and schedule and risk status and annual performance measures using, for example, earned value management (EVM).[10]

- **Collaboration.** Agile development emphasizes collaboration more than traditional approaches do. For example, to coordinate the many disciplines of an iteration, such as design and testing, customers work frequently and closely with technical staff. Furthermore, teams are often self-directed, meaning tasks and due dates are done within the team and coordinated with project sponsors and stakeholders as needed to complete the tasks. In contrast, with traditional project management, customer and technical staff typically work separately, and project tasks are prescribed and monitored by a project manager, who reports to entities such as a program management office.

See figure 1 for a depiction of Agile development compared to waterfall development.

Agile Frameworks

There are numerous frameworks available to Agile practitioners. One framework, called eXtreme Programming (XP), includes development techniques.[11] Another framework, called Scrum, defines management processes and roles. The Scrum framework is widely used in the public and private sector, and its terminology is often used in Agile discussions. For example, Scrum iterations are called sprints, which are bundled into releases. Sprint teams collaborate with minimal management direction, often co-located in work rooms. They meet daily and post their task status visibly, such as on wall charts.

Other concepts commonly used by sprint teams are user stories, story points, and backlog. User stories convey the customers' requirements. A user story typically follows the construct of "As a <type of user> I want <some goal> so that <some reason>." For example, "As a claims processor, I want to check a claim payment status so that I can promptly reply to a customer's request for payment status." Each user story is assigned a level of effort, called story points, which are a relative unit of measure used to communicate complexity and progress between the business and development sides of the project. To ensure that the product is usable at the end of every iteration, teams adhere to an agreed-upon definition of done. This includes stakeholders defining how completed work conforms to an organization's standards, conventions, and guidelines. The backlog is a list of user stories to be addressed by working software. If new requirements or defects are discovered, these can be stored in the backlog to be addressed in future iterations.

Progress in automating user stories is tracked daily using metrics and tools. An example of a metric is velocity. Velocity tracks the rate of work using the number of story points completed or expected to be completed in an iteration. For example, if a team completed 100 story points during a four-week iteration, the velocity for the team would be 100 story points every four weeks. An example of a tool is a burn-down chart, which tracks progress and the amount of work remaining for an iteration or for a release, which is made up of multiple iterations.

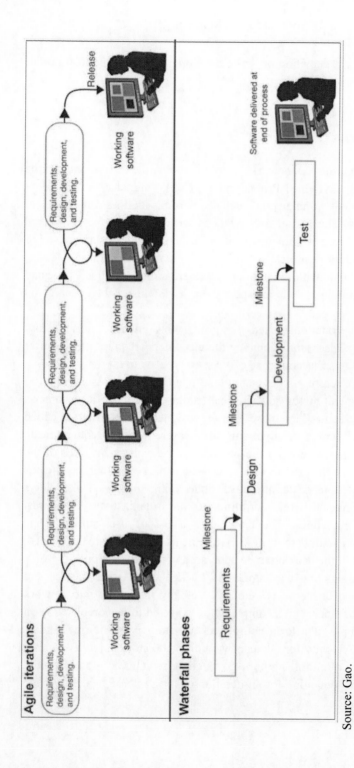

Source: Gao.

Figure 1. Comparison of Agile and Waterfall Development.

Agile in the Private and Federal Sectors

Agile use is reported in the private sector for small to medium sized projects and is starting to be used for larger projects as well. Also, widely accepted industry guidance on software development has recently been revised to include more Agile approaches. Specifically, the Software Engineering Institute's Capability Maturity Model® Integration[12] updated some process areas to help those using Agile to interpret its practices.

Furthermore, the federal government has begun to use Agile. For example, we have reported on several federal software development efforts that have used Agile techniques. Specifically, in December 2010 we reported[13] that the Department of Veterans Affairs was using Agile to develop software to support a new benefit for veterans. We also reported[14] that the Department of Defense was developing the Global Combat Support System-Joint system using Agile. In addition, the department sponsored studies that examined the possibility of more widespread use of Agile in its development projects.[15]

EFFECTIVE PRACTICES FOR APPLYING AGILE

We identified 32 practices and approaches[16] as effective for applying Agile to software development projects, based on an analysis of practices identified by experienced Agile users. Our analysis also found that the identified practices generally align with five key project management activities outlined in widely-accepted software development guidance: strategic planning, organizational commitment and collaboration, preparation, execution, and evaluation.

Strategic Planning

Strategic planning describes an organization's overall plans in an Agile environment. Six practices align with strategic planning. They are:

- **Strive to be more Agile, rather than simply following Agile methods and steps.** This approach encourages adoption of the philosophy, or mindset, rather than specific steps. This is also referred to as being Agile, or having agility versus using it.

- **Allow for a gradual migration to Agile appropriate to your readiness.** Migration steps might include combining Agile and existing methods, conducting pilots, and preparing technical infrastructure.

- **Observe and communicate with other organizations implementing Agile.** For example, those starting to use Agile can consult with others who have more experience, including academic, private sector, and federal practitioners.

- **Follow organizational change disciplines, such as establishing a sense of urgency and developing a change vision.** A clear vision of change helps staff understand what the organization is trying to achieve. Another organizational change discipline is communication strategies.

- **Be prepared for difficulties, regression, and negative attitudes.** This approach reinforces that Agile is not painless and users may backslide to entrenched software methods.

- **Start with Agile guidance and an Agile adoption strategy.** This practice advocates having these elements in place at the start, even if they must be copied from external sources.

Organizational Commitment and Collaboration

Organizational commitment describes the management actions that are necessary to ensure that a process is established and will endure. Collaboration in Agile typically refers to the close and frequent interaction of teams. Four practices align with organizational commitment and collaboration:

- **Ensure all components involved in Agile projects are committed to the organization's Agile approach.** This practice encourages organizations to ensure that everyone contributing to a project understands and commits to the organization's approach. This includes those working directly on the project and those with less direct involvement, such as those providing oversight.

- **Identify an Agile champion within senior management.** This practice calls for someone with formal authority within the organization to advocate the approach and resolve impediments at this level.

- **Ensure all teams include coaches or staff with Agile experience.** This practice stresses the importance of including on each team those with direct experience in applying Agile. While training is helpful, hands on experience helps the team members learn and adjust.
- **Empower small, cross-functional teams.** Empowered teams of 7 to 18 people decide what to deliver and how to produce it. The teams should not over-rely on one member's skills.

Preparation

Taking certain preparatory steps prior to the start of an iteration can facilitate a rapid development pace. The following eight practices generally align with the preparation of people and processes.

- **Train the entire organization in your Agile approach and mindset, and train Agile practitioners in your Agile methods.** For example, managers must understand the approach so that they know how it will affect them and teams need to know the specific steps of an iteration to conduct it properly.
- **Ensure that subject matter experts and business team members have the required knowledge.** This practice stresses that staff involved in fast-paced iterations must truly be experts in the processes being automated in that iteration in order to reduce delays. For example, a team member representing financial customers must be fully familiar with the needs of those customers.
- **Enhance migration to Agile concepts using Agile terms and examples.** For example, use terms like user stories instead of requirements, and Agile Center of Excellence instead of Project Management Office. Provide examples, such as one illustrating the small scope of a user story to teams writing these stories.
- **Create a physical environment conducive to collaboration.** A common practice is to co-locate the team in a single room where they can continually interact. Other ways to enhance collaboration are to reorganize office space and use tools to connect remote staff.
- **Identify measurable outcomes, not outputs, of what you want to achieve using Agile.** An example of this practice is creating a vision statement of project outcomes (such as a decrease in processing time

by a specific percent in a set time), rather than outputs (such as the amount of code produced).

- **Negotiate to adjust oversight requirements to a more Agile approach.** This practice notes that teams may be able to adjust oversight requirements by using frequent, tangible demonstrations to gain the trust of reviewers and investors, potentially reducing the need for more formal oversight documents.
- **Ensure that the definition of how a story will be determined to be done is comprehensive and objective.** Comprehensiveness includes defining what constitutes a finished product (i.e., packaged, documented, tested, and independently verified). Objective means measurable or verifiable versus subjective judgment.
- **Make contracts flexible to accommodate your Agile approach.** Contracts requiring waterfall-based artifacts and milestone reviews may not support the frequent changes and product demonstrations in iterations, and may inhibit adoption.

Execution

Execution entails the concrete steps necessary to conduct the iteration following the designated approach. The seven identified practices that align with execution are:

- **Use the same duration for each iteration.** An example would be establishing that iterations will be four weeks each within a release to establish a uniform pace.
- **Combine Agile frameworks such as Scrum and XP if appropriate.** Disciplines from different frameworks can be combined. For example, use project management disciplines from Scrum and technical practices from XP.
- **Enhance early customer involvement and design using test-driven development.** Test-driven development refers to writing software code to pass a test. This practice maintains that involving customers in these tests helps to engage them in the software development process.
- **Include requirements related to security and progress monitoring in your queue of unfinished work (backlog).** Including activities such as security reviews and status briefings in the backlog ensures

their time and cost are reflected and that they are addressed concurrent
with, and not after, iteration delivery.

- **Capture iteration defects in a tool such as a backlog.** This practice
  calls for queuing issues so that they are resolved in later iterations. For
  example, lists of unmet requirements generated at end-of-iteration
  demonstrations should be queued in the backlog for correction in a
  future iteration.
- **Expedite delivery using automated tools.** For example, tools can
  track software modifications, and compliant development sites or
  "sandboxes" help customers conceptualize the software in an
  environment that meets architectural and security standards.
- **Test early and often throughout the life cycle.** The theme of this
  practice is that testing during software code delivery instead of after
  delivery reduces risk and remediation costs.

Evaluation

Evaluations can occur at the project and organizational level. For example,
at the project level, the iteration is reviewed at its completion in a
retrospective. At the organizational level, processes are reviewed for
opportunities to improve the approach. The following seven practices align
with evaluation:

- **Obtain stakeholder/customer feedback frequently and closely.** For
  example, feedback is obtained during the iteration and at its
  completion at an iteration retrospective. This practice was linked to
  reducing risk, improving customer commitment, and improving
  technical staff motivation.
- **Continuously improve Agile adoption at both the project level
  and organization level.** This practice invokes the discipline of
  continuous improvement, meaning always looking for ways to
  improve. For example, improvements can be made by adding
  automated test and version control tools, and enhancing team rooms.
  These issues can be tracked in project and organizational-level
  backlogs.
- **Seek to identify and address impediments at the organization and
  project levels.** This practice encourages organizations to be frank
  about identifying impediments so that they can be addressed.

- **Determine project value based on customer perception and return on investment.** This practice recognizes that tracking progress only against cost or schedule criteria set before the project began could lead to inaccurate measurement of progress if, for example, major changes in scope occur. Instead, Agile encourages customer feedback as one measure of progress. Comparing solution value to the cost of the solution is also a gauge of success.
- **Gain trust by demonstrating value at the end of each iteration.** This practice includes demonstrating key requirements in early iterations, and showing customers that requirements in the backlog are delivered and not forgotten.
- **Track progress using tools and metrics.** Progress can be tracked using tools and metrics such as burn-down charts and velocity, which can be automated, and by success indicators such as "customer delight," and reduced staff stress and overtime.
- **Track progress daily and visibly.** This practice stresses that status is checked daily and publicly. For example, a progress chart is posted openly in the team's workspace, with timely revisions to reflect ongoing feedback.

Federal Use of Effective Practices

Officials who have used Agile on federal projects at five agencies generally agreed that the practices identified by the experienced users are effective in a federal setting.

Specifically, each practice was used and found effective by officials from at least one agency. Ten of the 32 practices were used and found effective by officials at all five agencies (see table 1).

Also, in most cases, a practice was still believed to be effective even if it was not used. For example, officials explained that they did not use a practice they indicated was effective because it was not appropriate for their project or that they used an alternate practice.

Although the identified practices were generally described as effective, officials from three agencies each reported one practice they had used but found to be not effective.

According to the agency officials, two practices were identified as ineffective because they were difficult to implement. These practices were: (1) ensuring commitment from components and (2) negotiating oversight requirements. The third practice, striving to be Agile rather than simply following Agile methods, was described by an agency official as not effective because he believed that strict adherence was necessary for a successful project.

FEDERAL CHALLENGES IN APPLYING AGILE

We identified 14 challenges with adapting to and applying Agile in the federal environment based on an analysis of experiences collected from five federal agencies that had applied Agile to a development effort. These challenges relate to significant differences in not only how software is developed but also how projects are managed in an Agile development environment versus a waterfall development environment.

We aligned the challenges with four of the project management activities used to organize effective practices: (1) ensuring organizational commitment and collaboration, (2) preparing for Agile, (3) executing development in an Agile environment, and (4) evaluating the product and project. In addition to identifying challenges, federal officials described efforts underway at their agencies to address these challenges.

Table 1. Practices Used and Found Effective by Five Agencies

Practice
1. Start with Agile guidance and an Agile adoption strategy.
2. Enhance migration to Agile concepts using Agile terms and examples.
3. Continuously improve Agile adoption at both project and organization levels.
4. Seek to identify and address impediments at the organization and project levels.
5. Obtain stakeholder/customer feedback frequently and closely.
6. Empower small, cross-functional teams.
7. Include requirements related to security and progress monitoring in your queue of unfinished work (backlog).
8. Gain trust by demonstrating value at the end of each iteration.
9. Track progress using tools and metrics.
10. Track progress daily and visibly.

Source: GAO.

Organizational Commitment and Collaboration

As described in the effective practices, Agile projects require the ongoing collaboration and commitment of a wide array of stakeholders, including business owners, developers, and security specialists. One way Agile promotes commitment and collaboration is by having teams work closely together, in one location, with constant team communication. Officials at the selected agencies identified challenges in achieving and maintaining such commitment and collaboration from their stakeholders as follows.

- **Teams had difficulty collaborating closely:** Officials from three agencies reported that teams were challenged in collaborating because staff were used to working independently. For example, one official reported that staff were challenged when asked to relocate to a team room because the technical staff preferred to work alone. The official added that some staff viewed open communication, such as posting project status on team room wall charts, as intrusive. A second official said that technical staff did not like constantly showing their work to customers. The third official said that customers initially did not want to see such development, preferring to wait for a polished product.

- **Teams had difficulty transitioning to self-directed work:** Officials at two agencies reported that staff had challenges in transitioning to self-directed teams. In Agile, teams made up of customers and technical staff are encouraged to create and manage their tasks without project manager direction and to elevate issues to stakeholders who have the authority to resolve them. Cross functionality is also encouraged to allow teams to share tasks. One official reported that teams used to direction from a project manager were challenged in taking responsibility for their work and in elevating issues they could not resolve within the team to senior officials. A second official noted that it was a challenge to create cross-functional teams because federal staff tend to be specialists in one functional area. An example of this would be where a team could include someone to represent system users, but that person may not be familiar with the needs of all users. Specifically, a team developing an insurance system might include someone with a background in claims processing. However, that person may not be experienced with payment procedures.

- **Staff had difficulty committing to more timely and frequent input:** While Agile advocates frequent input and feedback from all stakeholders, four agency officials noted challenges to commit to meeting such input expectations. One agency official noted that individuals were challenged to commit to keeping work products, such as schedules, updated to reflect the status of every iteration because they were not used to this rapid pace. A second official stated that teams initially had difficulty maintaining the pace of an iteration because they were used to stopping their work to address issues rather than making a decision and moving on. A third official said that it was challenging incorporating security requirements at the rapid pace of the sprint. A fourth official said customer availability was a challenge because customers initially did not understand the amount and pace of the time commitment for Agile and needed to develop a mindset to attend meetings as well as frequently review deliverables.

- **Agencies had trouble committing staff:** Three agency officials reported being challenged assigning and maintaining staff commitments to projects. The frequent input expected of staff involved in projects requires a more significant time commitment than that required for waterfall development projects that allow more sporadic participation. For example, two officials said their agencies were challenged dedicating staff with multiple, concurrent duties to teams because staff could not be spared from their other duties while participating in the Agile teams. The third official said stakeholder commitment is challenging to maintain when stakeholders rotate frequently and new staff need to learn the roles and responsibilities of those being replaced.

Preparation

When an organization following waterfall software development migrates to Agile, new tools and technical environments may be required to support that approach, as well as updates to guidance and procurement strategies. Officials described challenges in preparing for Agile as follows.

- **Timely adoption of new tools was difficult:** As identified in the effective practices, automated tools may be used to support project planning and reporting. One official noted that implementing Agile tools that aid in planning and reporting progress was initially a challenge because there was a delay in buying, installing, and learning to use these tools.

- **Technical environments were difficult to establish and maintain:** Two agency officials noted that establishing and maintaining technical environments posed challenges because Agile calls for development, test, and operational activities to be performed concurrently. According to one agency's officials, preparing and maintaining synchronized hardware and software environments for these three activities in time to support the releases was expensive to support and logistically challenging. Furthermore, one of these officials noted that his agency experienced a challenge running multiple concurrent iterations because this required more complex coordination of staff and resources.

- **Agile guidance was not clear:** Officials from three agencies identified a challenge related to the lack of clear guidance for Agile software development, particularly when agency software development guidance reflected a waterfall approach. For example, one official said that it was challenging to develop policy and procedure guidance for iterative projects because they were new, and the agency strategy aligned with the waterfall approach. As a result, it was difficult to ensure that iterative projects could follow a standard approach. A second official reported that deviating from waterfall-based procedural guidance to follow Agile methods made people nervous. For example, staff were nervous following team versus project manager directed tasks because this approach was not in their IT guidance. A third official said that their guidance mixed iterative and waterfall life cycle approaches, which staff found confusing.

- **Procurement practices may not support Agile projects:** Agile projects call for flexibility adding the staff and resources needed to meet each iteration, and to adapt to changes from one iteration to the next. One official stated that working with federal procurement practices presents a challenge where they do not support the flexibility required. For example, he said that federal contracts that require onerous, waterfall-based artifacts to constantly evaluate contractor performance are not needed in an Agile approach when the contractor is part of the team whose performance is based on the delivery of an iteration. Furthermore, the official said that they are challenged changing contractor staff in time to meet iteration time frames and that accommodating task changes from one iteration to the next is challenging because contracting officers require cumbersome traditional structured tasks and performance checks.

Execution

As described in the effective practices, Agile projects develop software iteratively, incorporating requirements and product development within an iteration. Such requirements may include compliance with agency legal and policy requirements. Officials reported challenges executing steps related to iterative development and compliance reviews as follows.

- **Customers did not trust iterative solutions:** Agile software products are presented to customers incrementally, for approval at the end of each iteration, instead of presenting complete products for approval at waterfall milestones. Officials at two agencies reported a challenge related to customer mistrust of iterative solutions. Specifically, one agency official said customers expecting a total solution feared that the initial demonstrations of functionality provided in the current iteration would be considered good enough, and they would not receive further software deliveries implementing the remainder of their requirements. At another agency, an official said this fear contributed to customers finding it difficult to define done. Specifically, customers were challenged in defining when each requirement would be considered done because they were afraid that this would be viewed as meaning all related functions were being met, and that unmet requirements would be dropped and never implemented.

- **Teams had difficulty managing iterative requirements:** Teams provide input on prioritizing requirements, and deciding what to do with new requirements discovered during iterations. Two agencies' officials reported challenges managing requirements. Specifically, one official reported that customers were initially challenged to validate and prioritize which requirements would be assigned to a release. Using the waterfall development model, they were used to identifying all requirements up front and not revisiting them as they were developed. The second official said they were challenged to accommodate new requirements within the fixed schedule for a product release.

- **Compliance reviews were difficult to execute within an iteration time frame:** Iterations may incorporate compliance reviews to ensure, for example, that agency legal and policy requirements are being met within the iteration. One agency official reported a challenge obtaining compliance reviews within the short, fixed time frame of an iteration because reviewers followed a slower waterfall schedule. Specifically, the official said that compliance reviewers queued requests as they arose and that the reviews could take months to perform. This caused delays for iterations that needed such reviews within the few weeks of the iteration.

Evaluation

Agile advocates evaluation of working software over the documentation and milestone reporting typical in traditional project management. Officials described challenges in evaluating projects related to the lack of alignment between Agile and traditional evaluation practices. Specifically, officials explained that:

- **Federal reporting practices do not align with Agile:** Two agency officials noted that several federal reporting practices do not align with Agile, creating challenges. For example, one official said federal oversight bodies want status reports at waterfall-based milestones rather than timely statements regarding the current state of the project. The second official said OMB's IT investment business case (known as the exhibit 300) and IT Dashboard, a publicly available website that displays detailed information on federal agencies' major IT investments,[17] are waterfall-based. For example, the IT Dashboard calls for monthly statistics instead of demonstrations of working software. He also noted that it is frustrating when dashboard statistics are flagged in red to note deviations, even when the deviation is positive, such as being ahead of schedule and under cost.
- **Traditional artifact reviews do not align with Agile:** Traditional oversight requires detailed artifacts in the beginning of a project, such as cost estimates and strategic plans, while Agile advocates incremental analysis. One agency official noted that requiring these

artifacts so early was challenging because it was more worthwhile to start with a high-level cost estimate and vision to be updated as the solution was refined through iterations, rather than spending time estimating costs and strategies that may change.

- **Traditional status tracking does not align with Agile:** Officials from three agencies noted that project status tracking in Agile does not align with traditional status tracking methods, creating challenges. For example, one official said that tracking the level of effort using story points instead of the traditional estimating technique based on hours was a challenge because team members were not used to that estimation method, although eventually this method was embraced. Two other agency officials said EVM was challenging to apply in an Agile environment. Specifically, one official said that the required use of EVM was challenging because there was no guidance on how to adapt it to iterations. The second official found EVM challenging because the agency was required to use it to track changes in cost, schedule, and product scope through monthly reports, and changes were viewed as control problems rather than as revisions to be expected during an iteration. For example, the project's scope was prioritized within every iteration based on the cost and schedule limits of the iteration and release. He also noted that risk tracking in Agile does not align with traditional risk tracking methods because issues are addressed within an iteration rather than queued, such as in a traditional monthly risk log.

In addition to identifying challenges, federal officials described their efforts to address these challenges. For example, officials said they clarify policies to address the challenge of Agile guidance lacking clarity. To mitigate the challenge related to customers not trusting iterative solutions, an official said they call the iteration review a mini-critical design review. This helps customers understand that they must declare the iteration complete or not, known as committing to done. Another official said one way that they addressed the challenge related to teams having difficulty managing iterative requirements was to add an empty iteration to the end of the release schedule to accommodate requirements discovered during the iterations.

In addition to the efforts at individual agencies to mitigate Agile challenges, the Federal CIO Council has begun an effort on a related topic. According to an official working with the Council, it is currently drafting a document on modular development. Consistent with OMB's IT reform efforts, the document is expected to provide guidance for agencies seeking to use more modular development approaches, such as Agile. However, according to the official, the draft does not specifically address Agile effective practices. Also, in June 2012 OMB released contracting guidance to support modular development.[18] This guidance includes factors for contracting officers to consider for modular development efforts regarding for example, statements of work, pricing arrangements, and small business opportunities.

CONCLUSION

As Agile methods begin to be more broadly used in federal development projects, agencies in the initial stages of adopting Agile can benefit from the knowledge of those with more experience. The ongoing effort by the Federal CIO Council to develop guidance on modular development provides an excellent opportunity to share these experiences. The effective practices and approaches identified in this report, as well as input from others with broad Agile experience, can inform this effort.

RECOMMENDATION FOR EXECUTIVE ACTION

To ensure that the experiences of those who have used Agile development are shared broadly, we recommend that the Federal CIO Council, working with its chair, the Office of Management and Budget's Deputy Director for Management, include practices such as those discussed in this report in the Council's ongoing effort to promote modular development in the federal government.

AGENCY COMMENTS AND OUR EVALUATION

We provided a draft of our report to OMB and to the five federal agencies included in our review. In oral comments on the draft, OMB's E-government program manager said that the draft recommendation was better addressed to the Federal CIO Council than to the OMB official who is the chair of the Council. Accordingly, we revised the recommendation to address it to the Council, working with its chair, the OMB Deputy Director for Management.

Two of the five agencies provided written comments on the draft. Specifically, the Department of Veterans Affairs Chief of Staff stated that the department generally agreed with the draft's findings, and the Acting Secretary of the Department of Commerce stated that the Patent and Trademark Office concurred with our assessment. Two other agencies, the Internal Revenue Service and the Department of Defense, provided technical comments via e-mail, which we incorporated as appropriate. In an e-mail, a manager in the National Aeronautics and Space Administration (NASA) center included in our review said that NASA had no comments.

David A. Powner
Director
Information Technology
Management Issues

Dr. Nabajyoti Barkakati
Director
Center for Technology and Engineering

APPENDIX I. OBJECTIVES, SCOPE, AND METHODOLOGY

Our objectives were to identify (1) effective practices in applying Agile for software development solutions and (2) federal challenges in implementing Agile development techniques.

To identify effective practices, we interviewed a nongeneralizable sample of nine experienced users and a tenth experienced user helped us pretest our data collection process.[19] To identify these users, we researched publications, attended forums, and obtained recommendations from federal and private officials knowledgeable about Agile. We selected individuals with Agile software development experience with public, private sector, and non-profit organizations. Using a structured interview, we asked them to identify effective practices when applying Agile methods to software development projects. We then compiled the reported practices and aligned and combined some with a broader practice. For example, practices related to preparation, such as mock and pilot iterations, were aligned and then combined into the final practice, "Allow for a gradual migration to Agile appropriate to your readiness." If a practice did not align with other or broader practices, it was listed individually.

We then sent the resulting list of practices in a questionnaire to our experienced users. This list was not organized into categories to ensure that each practice would be viewed individually. We asked our users to rate each practice as either (1) highly effective, (2) moderately effective, (3) somewhat effective, or (4) not applicable/do not know. We compiled the ratings and included in our list the practices that received at least six ratings of highly effective or moderately effective from the 8 experienced users who provided the requested ratings. [20] This resulted in 32 practices, which we aligned to key project management activities in Software Engineering Institute guidance: strategic planning, organizational commitment and collaboration, preparation, execution, and evaluation. This alignment was based on our best judgment.

To identify federal challenges, we interviewed officials responsible for five federal software development projects that reported using Agile practices. To identify the projects, we researched our previous work, federal websites, and publications, and attended federal forums. We selected a nongeneralizable sample of projects designed to reflect a range of agencies, system descriptions, and cost (see app. IV for details about the projects and the responsible officials). We then asked officials from each project to identify federal challenges in implementing an Agile approach using a structured interview. We summarized the challenges and categorized them as aligning with either organizational commitment and collaboration, preparation, execution, or evaluation.

Separately, we sent the federal officials a questionnaire listing the effective practices we compiled based on input from our experienced users. The questionnaire asked whether these practices were used and found effective. Although our results are not generalizable to the population of software development projects reporting the use of Agile practices, they provided valuable insight into both the effective use and challenges in applying Agile in the federal sector.

We conducted our work from October 2011 through July 2012 in accordance with all sections of GAO's Quality Assurance Framework that are relevant to our objectives.

The framework requires that we plan and perform the engagement to obtain sufficient and appropriate evidence to meet our stated objectives and to discuss any limitations in our work. We believe that the information obtained provides a reasonable basis for our findings and conclusions based on our audit objectives.

APPENDIX II. THE AGILE MANIFESTO AND PRINCIPLES

Agile development encompasses concepts that were previously used in software development. These concepts were documented as Agile themes and principles by 17 practitioners, who called themselves the Agile Alliance. In February 2001 the Alliance released "The Agile Manifesto,"[21] in which they declared: "We are uncovering better ways of developing software by doing it and helping others do it. Through this work we have come to value:

- individuals and interactions over processes and tools
- working software over comprehensive documentation
- customer collaboration over contract negotiation
- responding to change over following a plan."

The Alliance added that while they recognized the value in the second part of each statement (i.e., "processes and tools"), they saw more value in the first part ("individuals and interactions"). The Alliance further delineated their vision with twelve principles.

The 12 Agile Principles behind the Manifesto

- Our highest priority is to satisfy the customer through early and continuous delivery of valuable software.
- Welcome changing requirements, even late in development. Agile processes harness change for the customer's competitive advantage.
- Deliver working software frequently, from a couple of weeks to a couple of months, with a preference to the shorter timescale.
- Business people and developers must work together daily throughout the project.
- Build projects around motivated individuals. Give them the environment and support they need, and trust them to get the job done.
- The most efficient and effective method of conveying information to and within a development team is face-to-face conversation.
- Working software is the primary measure of progress.
- Agile processes promote sustainable development. The sponsors, developers, and users should be able to maintain a constant pace indefinitely.

- Continuous attention to technical excellence and good design enhances agility.
- Simplicity—the art of maximizing the amount of work not done—is essential.
- The best architectures, requirements, and designs emerge from self-organizing teams.
- At regular intervals, the team reflects on how to become more effective, then tunes and adjusts its behavior accordingly.

APPENDIX III. EXPERIENCED USERS

We interviewed the following experienced users to identify effective Agile practices. With one exception, they also contributed to the validation of our list of effective practices.

- Scott W. Ambler—Chief Methodologist for IT, IBM Rational
- Sanjiv Augustine—President, Lithespeed Consulting
- Gregor Bailar—Consultant
- Dr. Alan W. Brown—IBM Distinguished Engineer, Rational CTO for Europe, IBM Software Group
- Neil Chaudhuri—President, Vidya, L.L.C; Senior Software Engineer, Potomac Fusion
- Jerome Frese—Senior Enterprise Life Cycle Coach, Internal Revenue Service
- Dr. Steven J. Hutchison—Senior Executive, Office of the Secretary of Defense; Acquisition, Technology, and Logistics
- Mary Ann Lapham—Senior Member Technical Staff, Software Engineering Institute, Carnegie Mellon University
- Greg Pfister—Vice President Software Engineering, Agilex Technologies
- Bob Schatz—Senior Consultant and Advisor, Agile Infusion LLC

APPENDIX IV. FEDERAL PROJECT PROFILES

The five federal software development projects that reported challenges in applying Agile practices are profiled as follows.

Global Combat Support System-Joint Increment 7

Table 2. Profile of Global Combat Support System-J Increment 7

Agency	Department of Defense, Defense Information Systems Agency
System description	Supports logistics operations such as mission supplies for military personnel.
Agile approach	Scrum
Estimated cost	$192.3 million over a 5-year period
Officials interviewed included	Project and deputy project managers

Source: Agency data.

National Aeronautics and Space Administration Enterprise Applications Competency Center Materials Management Initiative

Table 3. Profile of National Aeronautics and Space Administration Enterprise Applications Competency Center Materials Management Initiative

Agency	National Aeronautics and Space Administration
System description	Supports receipt, warehousing, inventory, and issuance of operating materials and supplies.
Agile approach	Scrum
Estimated cost	$6.6 million
Officials interviewed included	Civilian project manager and manager in the National Aeronautics and Space Administration Enterprise Application Competency Center

Source: Agency data.

Patents End-to-End

Table 4. Profile of Patents End-to-End

Agency	Department of Commerce, Patent and Trademark Office
System description	Supports end-to-end electronic patent processing.
Agile approach	Scrum
Estimated cost	$150 million over 5 years
Officials interviewed included	Chief information officer, deputy chief information officer, patents portfolio manager, and other project managers

Source: Agency data.

Occupational Health Record-keeping System

Table 5. Profile of Occupational Health Record-keeping System

Agency	Department of Veterans Affairs, Veterans Health Administration
System description	Supports private employee health records.
Agile approach	Scrum
Estimated cost	$20 million for development and operation
Officials interviewed included	Current and previous IT project managers

Source: Agency data.

Affordable Care Act Branded Prescription Drugs

Table 6. Profile of Affordable Care Act Branded Prescription Drugs

Agency	Internal Revenue Service
System description	Supports pharmaceutical fee and payment tracking.
Agile approach	Iterative with some Agile practices
Estimated cost	$40 to $44M over 10 years
Officials interviewed included	Associate chief information officer and program manager

Source: Agency data.

End Notes

[1] GAO, *Information Management and Technology*, GAO/HR-97-9 (Washington, D.C.: February 1997) and *Information Technology: Critical Factors Underlying Successful Major Acquisitions*, GAO-12-7 (Washington, D.C.: Oct. 21, 2011).

[2] OMB, *25 Point Implementation Plan to Reform Federal Information Technology Management*, (Washington, D.C.: Dec. 9, 2010) and *Immediate Review of Financial Systems IT Projects*, M-10-26 (Washington, D.C.: June 28, 2010).

[3] Results from a nongeneralizable sample cannot be used to make inferences about a population. To mitigate this limitation, our sample was designed to ensure we obtained highly-qualified users with a broad range of Agile experience across the private, public, and non-profit sectors.

[4] See, for example, GAO, *Information Technology Reform: Progress Made: More Needs to Be Done to Complete Actions and Measure Results*, GAO-12-745T (Washington, D.C.: May 24, 2012); *FEMA: Action Needed to Improve Administration of the National Flood Insurance Program*, GAO-11-297 (Washington, D.C.: June 9, 2011); *Secure Border Initiative: DHS Needs to Reconsider Its Proposed Investment in Key Technology Program*, GAO-10-340 (Washington, D.C.: May 5, 2010); *Secure Border Initiative: DHS Needs to Address Testing and Performance Limitations That Place Key Technology Program at Risk*, GAO-10-158 (Washington, D.C.: Jan. 29, 2010); *Information Technology: Management and Oversight of Projects Totaling Billions of Dollars Need Attention*, GAO-09-624T

(Washington, D.C.: Apr. 28, 2009); *Information Technology: Agriculture Needs to Strengthen Management Practices for Stabilizing and Modernizing Its Farm Program Delivery Systems*, GAO-08-657 (Washington, D.C.: May 16, 2008); *Information Technology: FBI Following a Number of Key Acquisition Practices on New Case Management System, but Improvements Still Needed*, GAO-07-912 (Washington, D.C.: July 30, 2007); *Information Technology: Foundational Steps Being Taken to Make Needed FBI Systems Modernization Management Improvements*, GAO-04-842 (Washington, D.C.: Sept.10, 2004); and GAO/HR-97-9.

[5] We recently reported on OMB's progress on these reforms in GAO, *Information Technology Reform: Progress Made; More Needs to Be Done to Complete Actions and Measure Results*, GAO-12-461 (Washington, D.C.: Apr. 26, 2012).

[6] The Agile Manifesto was written by a group of methodologists called the Agile Alliance. For more information on the creation of the Agile Manifesto, go to http://agilemanifesto.org.

[7] For example, see the comparison of Agile and waterfall in Carnegie Mellon Software Engineering Institute, Mary Ann Lapham, et al., *Considerations for Using Agile in DOD Acquisition* (Pittsburgh, Pa: April 2010).

[8] GAO, *Information Technology Investment Management: A Framework for Assessing and Improving Process Maturity*, GAO-04-394G (Washington, D.C.: March 2004).

[9] For certain IT investments, OMB requires an annual report called the exhibit 300 and monthly status on a website called the IT Dashboard (http://www.itdashboard.gov/).

[10] EVM is a tool for measuring a project's progress by comparing the value of work accomplished with the amount of work expected to be completed, and is based on variances from cost and schedule baselines.

[11] For example, XP includes technical practices such as test-driven development, in which the test of software code to meet a requirement is written before writing the operational code.

[12] The Software Engineering Institute is a nationally recognized, federally funded research and development center established at Carnegie Mellon University to address software engineering practices. The institute has developed process maturity models for software development, including CMMI® for Development, Version 1.3, *Improving Processes for Developing Better Products and Services*, (Pittsburgh, Pa: November 2010).

[13] GAO, *Information Technology: Veterans Affairs Can Further Improve Its Development Process for Its New Education Benefits System*, GAO-11-115 (Washington, D.C.: Dec. 1, 2010).

[14] GAO-12-7.

[15] Carnegie Mellon Software Engineering Institute, Mary Ann Lapham, et al., *Considerations for Using Agile in DOD Acquisition* (Pittsburgh, Pa: April 2010); and *Agile Methods: Selected DOD Management and Acquisition Concerns* (Pittsburgh, Pa: October 2011).

[16] Although we asked the experienced users to identify effective practices, several of the items they identified can be considered more of an approach, or way to think about proceeding, than practices that describe how something should be done. This aligns with the concept of Agile being as much a philosophy as a set of steps to be followed.

[17] The IT Dashboard includes assessments of actual performance against cost and schedule targets (referred to as ratings) for approximately 800 major federal IT investments. The IT Dashboard website is located at http://www.itdashboard.gov/.

[18] OMB, *Contracting Guidance to Support Modular Development* (Washington, D.C.: June 2012).

[19] Results from nongeneralizable samples cannot be used to make inferences about a population. To mitigate this limitation, our sample was designed to ensure we obtained highly-qualified users with a broad range of Agile experience across the private, public, and non-profit sectors.

[20] The ninth experienced user was asked for input on the list of practices with the others, but did not respond in time to meet our reporting deadline.

[21] http://agilemanifesto.org.

In: Information Technology
Editor: Fedele D'Onofrio

ISBN: 978-1-62417-641-8
© 2013 Nova Science Publishers, Inc.

Chapter 3

INFORMATION TECHNOLOGY REFORM: PROGRESS MADE; MORE NEEDS TO BE DONE TO COMPLETE ACTIONS AND MEASURE RESULTS[*]

United States Government Accountability Office

WHY GAO DID THIS STUDY

While investments in IT have the potential to improve lives and organizations, federal IT projects too often experience cost overruns, schedule slippages, and performance shortfalls. To address acquisition challenges, improve operational efficiencies, and deliver more value to the American taxpayer, in December 2010, OMB's Federal CIO issued a 25-point IT Reform Plan.

GAO was asked to (1) evaluate the progress OMB and key federal agencies have made on selected action items in the IT Reform Plan, (2) assess the plans for addressing action items that are behind schedule, and (3) assess the extent to which sound measures are in place to evaluate the success of the IT reform initiatives.

To do so, GAO selected 10 of the 25 action items from the IT Reform Plan, focusing on the more important activities due to be completed by

---

[*] This is an edited, reformatted and augmented version of the Highlights of GAO-12-461, a report to congressional requesters, dated April 2012.

December 2011; analyzed agency documentation; and interviewed agency officials.

WHAT GAO RECOMMENDS

GAO is making recommendations to three agencies to complete key IT Reform action items; the agencies generally concurred. GAO is also making recommendations to OMB to complete key action items, accurately characterize the items' status, and establish measures for IT reform initiatives. OMB agreed to complete key action items, but disagreed with the latter recommendations, noting that the agency believes it is characterizing the items' status correctly and that measures are not warranted. GAO maintains that its recommendations are valid.

WHAT GAO FOUND

The Office of Management and Budget (OMB) and key federal agencies have made progress on action items in the Information Technology (IT) Reform Plan, but there are several areas where more remains to be done. Of the 10 key action items GAO reviewed, 3 were completed and 7 were partially completed by December 2011, in part because the initiatives are complex (see table).

OMB reported greater progress than GAO determined, stating that 7 of the 10 action items were completed and that 3 were partially completed. While OMB officials acknowledge that there is more to do in each of the topic areas, they consider the key action items to be completed because the IT Reform Plan has served its purpose as a catalyst for a set of broader initiatives. They explained that work will continue on all of the initiatives even after OMB declares that the related action items are completed under the IT Reform Plan. We disagree with this approach. In prematurely declaring the action items to be completed, OMB risks losing momentum on the progress it has made to date.

Until OMB and the agencies complete the action items, the benefits of the reform initiatives—including increased operational efficiencies and more effective management of large-scale IT programs—will likely be delayed.

GAO Assessment of Selected IT Reform Plan Action Items

Data center consolidation	◑	Guidance on modular development	◑
Cloud computing	◑	Budget models for modular development	◑
Contract vehicle for infrastructure	●	Routine IT purchases under agency CIO	◑
Best practices platform	◑	Investment review boards	●
IT acquisition professionals	●	Role of agency CIO and CIO Council	◑

Source: GAO analysis of OMB and agency data. Key: ● = Completed, ◑ = Partially completed

OMB and key agencies plan to continue efforts to address the seven items that GAO identified as behind schedule, but lack time frames for completing most of them. For example, OMB plans to work with congressional committees during the fiscal year 2013 budget process to assist in exploring legislative proposals to establish flexible budget models and to consolidate certain routine IT purchases under agency chief information officers (CIO). However, OMB has not established time frames for completing five of the seven IT Reform Plan action items that are behind schedule. Until OMB and the agencies establish time frames for completing these corrective actions, they increase the risk that key action items will not be completed or effectively managed to closure. Further, they diminish the likelihood of achieving the full benefits of IT reform.

OMB has not established performance measures for evaluating the results of most of the IT reform initiatives GAO reviewed. Specifically, OMB has established performance measures for 4 of the 10 action items, including data center consolidation and cloud computing. However, no performance measures exist for 6 other action items, including establishing the best practices collaboration platform and developing a cadre of IT acquisition professionals. Until outcome-oriented performance measures are in place for each of the action items, OMB will be limited in its ability to evaluate progress that has been made and to determine whether or not the initiative is achieving its intended results.

ABBREVIATIONS

CIO   Chief Information Officer
GSA   General Services Administration
IT   information technology
NIST   National Institute of Standards and Technology

OFPP	Office of Federal Procurement Policy
OMB	Office of Management and Budget
OPM	Office of Personnel Management

April 26, 2012

The Honorable Joseph I. Lieberman
Chairman
The Honorable Susan M. Collins
Ranking Member
Committee on Homeland Security and Governmental Affairs
United States Senate

The Honorable Thomas R. Carper
Chairman
Subcommittee on Federal Financial Management,
Government Information, Federal Services, and International Security
Committee on Homeland Security and Governmental Affairs
United States Senate

In December 2010, the Federal Chief Information Officer (CIO) released a 25-point plan for reforming federal information technology (IT) management.[1] This document established an ambitious plan for achieving operational efficiencies and effectively managing large-scale IT programs. It also clearly identified actions to be completed in three different time frames: (1) within 6 months (by June 2011), (2) between 6 and 12 months (by December 2011), and (3) between 12 and 18 months (by June 2012).

To understand how agencies are implementing the IT Reform Plan, you asked us to (1) evaluate the progress the Office of Management and Budget (OMB) and key federal agencies have made on selected action items in the IT Reform Plan, (2) assess the plans for addressing any action items that are behind schedule, and (3) assess the extent to which sound measures are in place to evaluate the success of the IT reform initiatives.

To do so, we selected 10 action items from the IT Reform Plan, focusing on action items that (1) were expected to be completed by December 2011, (2) covered multiple different topic areas, and (3) were considered by internal and OMB subject matter experts to be the more important items. We also selected three federal agencies (the Departments of Homeland Security, Justice, and

Veterans Affairs) based on several factors, including high levels of IT spending and large numbers of investments in fiscal year 2011. We then evaluated the steps OMB and the three federal agencies had taken to implement the selected action items from the IT Reform Plan. In cases where the action was behind schedule, we compared plans for addressing the schedule shortfalls to sound project planning practices.[2] We also determined whether and how agencies were tracking performance measures associated with these action items, and compared these measures to best practices in IT performance management.[3] In addition, we interviewed OMB and selected agency officials regarding progress, plans, and measures.

We conducted this performance audit from August 2011 to April 2012 in accordance with generally accepted government auditing standards. Those standards require that we plan and perform the audit to obtain sufficient, appropriate evidence to provide a reasonable basis for our findings and conclusions based on our audit objectives. We believe that the evidence obtained provides a reasonable basis for our findings and conclusions based on our audit objectives. See appendix I for a complete description of our objectives, scope, and methodology.

BACKGROUND

IT can enrich people's lives and improve organizational performance. For example, during the last two decades the Internet has matured from being a means for academics and scientists to communicate with each other to a national resource where citizens can interact with their government in many ways, such as by receiving services, supplying and obtaining information, asking questions, and providing comments on proposed rules.

While investments in IT have the potential to improve lives and organizations, some federally funded IT projects can—and have— become risky, costly, unproductive mistakes. As we have described in numerous reports and testimonies, federal IT projects too frequently incur cost overruns and schedule slippages while contributing little to mission-related outcomes. Further, while IT should enable government to better serve the American people, the federal government has not achieved expected productivity improvements—despite spending more than $600 billion on IT over the past decade.

Roles and Responsibilities for Federal IT Management

Over the last two decades, Congress has enacted several laws to assist agencies and the federal government in managing IT investments. Key laws include the Paperwork Reduction Act of 1995,[4] the Clinger-Cohen Act of 1996,[5] and the E-Government Act of 2002.[6]

Also, the GPRA (Government Performance and Results Act) Modernization Act of 2010 includes IT management as a priority goal for improving the federal government.[7]

- *Paperwork Reduction Act of 1995.* The act specifies OMB and agency responsibilities for managing information resources, including the management of IT.

  Among its provisions, this law establishes agency responsibility for maximizing the value and assessing and managing the risks of major information systems initiatives. It also requires that OMB develop and oversee policies, principles, standards, and guidelines for federal agency IT functions, including periodic evaluations of major information systems.

- *Clinger-Cohen Act of 1996.* The act places responsibility for managing investments with the heads of agencies and establishes CIOs to advise and assist agency heads in carrying out this responsibility. Additionally, this law requires OMB to establish processes to analyze, track, and evaluate the risks and results of major capital investments in information systems made by federal agencies and report to Congress on the net program performance benefits achieved as a result of these investments.

- *E-Government Act of 2002.* The act establishes a federal e-government initiative, which encourages the use of web-based Internet applications to enhance the access to and delivery of government information and services to citizens, business partners, employees, and agencies at all levels of government. The act also requires OMB to report annually to Congress on the status of e-government initiatives.

  In these reports, OMB is to describe the administration's use of e-government principles to improve government performance and the delivery of information and services to the public.

- *GPRA (Government Performance and Results Act) Modernization Act of 2010.* The act establishes a new framework aimed at taking a more crosscutting and integrated approach to focusing on results and improving government performance. It requires OMB, in coordination with agencies, to develop long-term, outcome-oriented goals for a limited number of crosscutting policy areas at least every four years. The act specifies that these goals should include five areas: financial management, human capital management, IT management, procurement and acquisition management, and real property management.[8]

On an annual basis, OMB is to provide information on how these long-term crosscutting goals will be achieved.

As set out in these laws, OMB is to play a key role in helping federal agencies manage their investments by working with them to better plan, justify, and determine how much they need to spend on projects and how to manage approved projects.

Within OMB, the Office of E-government and Information Technology, headed by the Federal CIO, directs the policy and strategic planning of federal IT investments and is responsible for oversight of federal technology spending.

In addition, the Office of Federal Procurement Policy (OFPP) is responsible for shaping the policies and practices federal agencies use to acquire the goods and services they need to carry out their missions.

Agency CIOs are also expected to have a key role in IT management. Federal law, specifically the Clinger-Cohen Act, has defined the role of the CIO as the focal point for IT management, requiring agency heads to designate CIOs to lead reforms that would help control system development risks; better manage technology spending; and achieve real, measurable improvements in agency performance.

In addition, the CIO Council—comprised of the CIOs and Deputy CIOs of 28 agencies and chaired by OMB's Deputy Director for Management—is the principal interagency forum for improving agency practices related to the design, acquisition, development, modernization, use, sharing, and performance of federal information resources.

The CIO Council is responsible for developing recommendations for overall federal IT management policy, sharing best practices, including the development of performance measures, and identifying opportunities and sponsoring cooperation in using information resources.

Table 1. OMB's IT Reform Plan: Action Items, Required Activities, and Responsible Parties

Plan number	Action item title	Required activities	Responsible parties	Due date
1	Complete detailed implementation plans to consolidate 800 data centers by 2015	• Complete consolidation plans that include a technical roadmap, clear consolidation targets, and measurable milestones • Identify dedicated agency-specific program managers • Establish a cross-government task force comprised of the agency program managers • Ensure the task force meets monthly • Launch a public dashboard for tracking progress towards closures	OMB and federal agencies	June 2011
2	Create a governmentwide marketplace for data center availability	• Establish a governmentwide marketplace for agencies to market or obtain data center services	OMB and GSA	June 2012
3	Shift to a "cloud first" policy	• Establish a federal strategy for moving to cloud computing[a] • Identify three services (per agency) that are to move to cloud computing • Establish migration plans for the three services that are to move • Fully migrate the first service within 12 months	OMB and federal agencies	June 2011
4	Stand-up contract vehicles for secure Infrastructure-as-a-Service[b] solutions	• Make a common set of contract vehicles for secure cloud-based infrastructure solutions available governmentwide	GSA	June 2011
5	Stand-up contract vehicles for commodity services[c]	• Make contract vehicles for cloud-based e-mail solutions available governmentwide	GSA	December 2011
6	Develop a strategy for shared services	• Establish a vision and benchmarks for sharing services among federal agencies	CIO Council	December 2011
7	Design a formal IT program management career path	• Create a specialized career path for IT program managers that focuses on experience and expertise • Provide agencies authority to directly hire IT program managers • Have agencies identify and plan to fill competency gaps in IT program management	OPM and OMB	June 2011
8	Scale IT program management career path	• Expand IT program management career paths across the federal government	OPM and federal agencies	June 2012

Plan number	Action item title	Required activities	Responsible parties	Due date
9	Require integrated program teams	• Issue guidance requiring integrated program teams for all major IT programs • Dedicate resources throughout the program • Make program team members accountable for individual goals and overall program success	OMB	June 2011
10	Launch a best practices collaboration platform	• Establish a portal for program managers to exchange information on best practices • Require agencies to submit their experiences to the portal • Codify and synthesize agency submissions to provide a searchable database that facilitates real-time problem solving	CIO Council	June 2011
11	Launch technology fellows program	• Create a technology fellows program and the accompanying recruiting infrastructure to allow the government to tap into the emerging talent pool at universities with well-recognized technology programs	CIO Council	December 2011
12	Enable IT program manager mobility across government and industry	• Develop a process to encourage the movement of program managers across the government and industry in order to leverage their knowledge and expertise • Design opportunities for federal program managers to rotate through industry • Establish a repository of information on all federal government IT program managers	OMB, CIO Council, and OPM	June 2012
13	Design a cadre of specialized IT acquisition professionals[d]	• Define an IT acquisition specialist position • Establish the requirements, guidance, curriculum, and process for becoming one • Create guidance to strengthen the IT acquisition skills and capabilities of IT acquisition specialists	OMB and federal agencies	June 2011
14	Identify IT acquisition best practices and adopt governmentwide	• Study the experience of agencies with specialized IT acquisition teams • Develop a model for implementing such teams governmentwide	OFPP	June 2011
15	Issue contracting guidance and templates to support modular development	• Work with IT and acquisition community to develop guidance on contracting for modular development[e] • Obtain feedback from industry leaders • Develop templates and samples supporting modular development	OFPP	December 2011

Table 1. (Continued)

Plan number	Action item title	Required activities	Responsible parties	Due date
16	Reduce barriers to entry for small innovative technology companies	• Take steps to develop clearer and more comprehensive policies for government contracting with small businesses	Small Business Administration, GSA, and OFPP	June 2012
17	Work with Congress to create IT budget models that align with modular development	• Analyze working capital funds and transfer authorities to identify current IT budget flexibilities • Identify programs at agencies where additional budget flexibilities could improve outcomes • Work with Congress to propose budgetary models to complement the modular development approach • Evaluate mechanisms for increased transparency for these programs	OMB and federal agencies	June 2011
18	Develop supporting materials and guidance for flexible IT budget models	• Develop a set of best practices and materials that explain the need for budget flexibilities and prescribe a path to achieve more flexible budget models	OMB, Chief Financial Officer Council, and CIO Council	December 2011
19	Work with Congress to scale flexible IT budget models more broadly	• Work with Congress to launch flexible IT budget models at selected agencies • Extend these budget models across the government as successes are demonstrated	OMB and federal agencies	June 2012
20	Work with Congress to consolidate commodity IT spending under agency CIO	• Work with Congress to consolidate commodity IT spending under the agency CIO • Develop a workable funding model for "commodity" IT services • Have the CIO Council and agency CIOs identify "commodity" services to be included in this funding model as they are migrated towards shared services	OMB and federal agencies	June 2011
21	Reform and strengthen Investment Review Boards	• Revamp IT budget submissions • Have agencies conduct "TechStat" reviews[f] • Have OMB analysts provide training to agency CIOs in the "TechStat" methodology	OMB and federal agencies	June 2011
22	Redefine role of agency CIOs and CIO Council	• Make agency CIOs responsible for managing the portfolio of large IT projects within their agencies	Federal CIO and agency CIOs	June 2011

Plan number	Action item title	Required activities	Responsible parties	Due date
23	Roll out "TechStat" model at a component level	• Have the CIO Council periodically review the highest priority "TechStat" findings assembled by the agency CIOs • Have an agency component organizations conduct "TechStat" reviews • Make agency CIOs responsible for deploying the necessary tools and training on how to conduct "TechStat" reviews	Agency CIOs com	June 2012
24	Launch "myth-busters" education campaign	• Identify the major myths that hinder the acquisition process • Reach out to key stakeholders in industry and government to dispel the myths	OFPP	June 2011
25	Launch an interactive platform for agency-industry collaboration before requests for proposals are issued	• Launch a governmentwide, online, interactive platform for identifying inexpensive, efficient solutions in the period prior to issuing a request for proposals	GSA	June 2011

Source: GAO analysis of OMB's IT Reform Plan.

Note: The shaded items are those reviewed in this report.

[a] Cloud computing is an emerging form of computing where users have access to scalable, on-demand capabilities that are provided through Internet-based technologies. It has the potential to provide IT services more quickly and at a lower cost.

[b] Infrastructure-as-a-Service is one type of cloud computing in which a vendor offers various infrastructure components such as hardware, storage, and other fundamental computing resources.

[c] Commodity services are systems or services used to carry out routine tasks (e.g., e-mail, data centers, and web infrastructure).

[d] While the IT Reform Plan discusses having agencies develop cadres of specialists, there is no requirement for agencies to do so.

[e] According to the IT Reform Plan, modular development is a system development technique that delivers functionality in shorter time frames by creating requirements at a high level and then refining them through an iterative process, with extensive engagement and feedback from stakeholders.

[f] OMB defines a TechStat as a face-to-face, evidence-based accountability review of an IT investment that results in concrete actions to address weaknesses and reduces wasteful spending by turning around troubled programs and terminating failed programs.

Federal IT Reform Plan Strives to Address Persistent Challenges

After assessing the most persistent challenges in acquiring, managing, and operating IT systems, in December 2010, the Federal CIO established a 25-point IT Reform Plan designed to address challenges in IT acquisition, improve operational efficiencies, and deliver more IT value to the American taxpayer.[9]

The actions were planned to be completed in three different time frames: (1) within 6 months (by June 2011), (2) between 6 and 12 months (by December 2011), and (3) between 12 and 18 months (by June 2012). Several different organizations were assigned ownership of the key action items, including the Federal CIO, the CIO Council, the General Services Administration (GSA), Office of Personnel Management (OPM), OFPP, the Small Business Administration, and other federal agencies.

Table 1 contains detailed information on the action items in the IT Reform Plan. Shaded items are those selected for review in this report.

GAO Has Previously Reported on Needed Improvements in Federal IT Management

Given the challenges that federal agencies have experienced in acquiring and managing IT investments, we have issued a series of reports aimed at improving federal IT management over the last decade.

Our reports cover a variety of topics, including data center consolidation, cloud computing, CIO responsibilities, system acquisition challenges, and modular development. Key reports that address topics covered in the IT Reform Plan include:

- *Data center consolidation.* In July 2011, we reported on the status of OMB's federal data center consolidation initiative.[10] Under this initiative, OMB required 24 participating agencies to submit data center inventories and consolidation plans by the end of August 2010. However, we found that only one of the agencies submitted a complete data center inventory and no agency submitted a complete data center consolidation plan.

  We concluded that until these inventories and plans are complete, agencies might not be able to implement their consolidation activities and realize expected cost savings. We recommended that agencies complete the missing elements in their plans and inventories. In response to our recommendations, in October and November 2011, the agencies updated their inventories and plans. We have ongoing work assessing the agencies' revised plans, and in February 2012, we reported that our preliminary assessment of the updated plans showed that not all agency plans were updated to include all required information.[11]

- *Cloud computing.* In May 2010, we reported on multiple agencies' efforts to ensure the security of governmentwide cloud computing. We noted that while OMB, GSA, and the National Institute of Standards and Technology (NIST) had initiated efforts to ensure secure cloud computing, significant work remained to be completed.[12] For example, OMB had not yet finished a cloud computing strategy; GSA had begun a procurement for expanding cloud computing services, but had not yet developed specific plans for establishing a shared information security assessment and authorization process; and NIST had not yet issued cloud-specific security guidance. We made several recommendations to address these issues.

Specifically, we recommended that OMB establish milestones to complete a strategy for federal cloud computing and ensure it addressed information security challenges. OMB subsequently published a strategy which addressed the importance of information security when using cloud computing, but did not fully address several key challenges confronting agencies.

We also recommended that GSA consider security in its procurement for cloud services, including consideration of a shared assessment and authorization process. GSA has since developed an assessment and authorization process for systems shared among federal agencies. Finally, we recommended that NIST issue guidance specific to cloud computing security. NIST has since issued multiple publications which address such guidance.

More recently, in October 2011, we testified that 22 of 24 major federal agencies reported that they were either concerned or very concerned about the potential information security risks associated with cloud computing. [13] These risks include being dependent on the security practices and assurances of vendors and the sharing of computing resources.

We stated that these risks may vary based on the cloud deployment model. Private clouds, whereby the service is set up specifically for one organization, may have a lower threat exposure than public clouds, whereby the service is available to any paying customer. Evaluating this risk requires an examination of the specific security controls in place for the cloud's implementation.

We also reported that the CIO Council had established a cloud computing Executive Steering Committee to promote the use of cloud computing in the federal government, with technical and administrative support provided by GSA's Cloud Computing Program Management Office, but had not finalized key processes or guidance. A subgroup of this committee had developed the Federal Risk and Authorization Management Program, a governmentwide program to provide joint authorizations and continuous security monitoring services for all federal agencies, with an initial focus on cloud computing.

The subgroup had worked with its members to define interagency security requirements for cloud systems and services and related information security controls.

- *Best practices in IT acquisition.* In October 2011, we reported on best practices in IT acquisitions in the federal government.[14] Specifically, we identified nine factors critical to the success of three or more of seven IT investments.[15]

  The factors most commonly identified include active engagement of stakeholders, program staff with the necessary knowledge and skills, and senior department and agency executive support for the program. We reported that while these factors will not necessarily ensure that federal agencies will successfully acquire IT systems because many different factors contribute to successful acquisitions, they may help federal agencies address the well-documented acquisition challenges they face.

- *IT spending authority.* In February 2008, we reported that the Department of Veterans Affairs had taken important steps toward a more disciplined approach to ensuring oversight of and accountability for the department's IT budget and resources.[16] These steps included providing the department's CIO responsibility for ensuring that there are controls over the budget and for overseeing all capital planning and execution, and designating leadership to assist in overseeing functions such as portfolio management.

- *Investment review and oversight.* During the past several years, we issued numerous reports and testimonies on OMB's initiatives to highlight troubled IT projects.[17]

We made multiple recommendations to OMB and federal agencies to enhance the oversight and transparency of federal IT projects. For example, in 2005 we recommended that OMB develop a central list of projects and their deficiencies, and analyze that list to develop governmentwide and agency assessments of the progress and risks of the investments, identifying opportunities for continued improvement.[18] In 2006, we recommended that OMB develop a single aggregate list of high-risk projects and their deficiencies and use that list to report to Congress on progress made in correcting high-risk problems.[19]

As a result, OMB started publicly releasing aggregate data on its internal list of mission-critical projects that needed to improve (called its Management Watch List) and disclosing the projects' deficiencies. The agency also established a High-Risk List, which consisted of projects identified as requiring special attention from oversight authorities and the highest levels of agency management.

In June 2009, to further improve the transparency and oversight of agencies' IT investments, OMB publicly deployed a website, known as the IT Dashboard, which replaced its Management Watch List and High-Risk List. The data in the IT Dashboard is drawn from federal agencies' budget submissions. [20] OMB analysts use the IT Dashboard to identify IT investments that are experiencing performance problems and to select them for a TechStat session—a review of selected IT investments between OMB and agency leadership that is led by the Federal CIO.

We have since completed three successive reviews of the data on the IT Dashboard and reported that while it is an important tool for reporting and monitoring major IT projects, the cost and schedule ratings were not always accurate for selected agencies.[21] We made recommendations to improve the accuracy of the data and, in our most recent report, found that the accuracy had improved.

In addition, in September 2011, we reported that OMB provides guidance to agencies on how to report on their IT investments, but this guidance does not ensure complete reporting or facilitate the identification of duplicative investments. [22] We recommended that OMB clarify its reporting on IT investments and improve its guidance to agencies on identifying and categorizing IT investments. OMB did not agree that further efforts were needed to clarify reporting and has not yet addressed our recommendations. Given the importance of continued improvement in OMB's reporting and guidance, we maintain that the recommendations are warranted.

- *Agency CIO responsibilities.* In September 2011, we reported that the responsibilities of the CIOs differ among agencies, and that CIOs face limitations in exercising their influence in certain IT management areas. [23] Specifically, CIOs do not always have sufficient control over IT investments, and they often have limited influence over the IT workforce, such as in hiring and firing decisions and the performance of component-level CIOs. We noted that more consistent implementation of CIOs' authority could enhance their effectiveness in these areas and that while OMB had taken steps to increase CIOs' effectiveness, it had not established measures of accountability to ensure that responsibilities are fully implemented. We recommended that OMB update its guidance to establish measures of accountability for ensuring that CIOs' responsibilities are fully implemented and require agencies to establish internal processes for documenting lessons learned. OMB officials generally agreed with our recommendations and, in August 2011, issued a memo to agencies emphasizing the CIO's role in driving the investment review process and responsibility over the entire IT portfolio for an agency. [24] The memo identified four areas in which the CIO should have a lead role: IT governance, program management, commodity services, and information security.

OMB AND KEY FEDERAL AGENCIES HAVE MADE PROGRESS ON IT REFORM ACTION ITEMS, BUT MUCH REMAINS TO BE DONE

OMB and key federal agencies have made progress on selected action items identified in the IT Reform Plan, but there are several areas where more remains to be done. Of the 10 key action items we reviewed, 3 were completed and the other 7 were partially completed by December 2011. The action items that are behind schedule share a common reason for the delays: the complexity of the initiatives. In all seven of the cases, OMB and the federal agencies are still working on the initiatives.

In a December 2011 progress report on its IT Reform Plan, OMB reported that it made greater progress than we determined. The agency reported that of the 10 action items, 7 were completed and 3 were partially completed. OMB officials from the Office of E-government and Information Technology explained that the reason for the difference in assessments is that they believe that the IT Reform Plan has served its purpose in acting as a catalyst for a set of broader initiatives. They noted that work will continue on all of the initiatives even after OMB declares the related action items to be completed under the IT Reform Plan.

We disagree with this approach. In prematurely declaring the action items to be completed, OMB risks losing momentum on the progress it has made to date. Table 2 provides both OMB's and our assessments of the status of the key action items, with action items rated as "completed" if all of the required activities identified in the reform plan were completed, and "partially completed" if some, but not all, of the required activities were completed. Until OMB and the agencies complete the action items called for in the IT Reform Plan, the benefits of the reform initiatives—including increased operational efficiencies and more effective management of large-scale IT programs—may be delayed. With the last of the action items in the IT Reform Plan due to be completed by June 2012, it will be important for OMB and the agencies to ensure that the action items due at earlier milestones are completed as soon as possible.

OMB AND KEY AGENCIES PLAN TO ADDRESS ITEMS THAT WE FOUND TO BE BEHIND SCHEDULE, BUT LACK DEFINED TIME FRAMES FOR COMPLETING THEM

According to leading practices in industry and government, effective planning is critical to successfully managing a project. Effective project planning includes taking corrective actions when project deliverables fall behind schedule and defining time frames for completing the corrective actions.[25] As noted earlier in this report, we identified seven action items that are behind schedule or falling short of the IT Reform Plan's requirements.

Table 2. GAO's Assessment of the Status of Key Action Items

Plan number and action item title	OMB's reported status (as of December 2011)	GAO's assessment	Description
(1) Complete detailed implementation plans to consolidate at least 800 data centers by 2015	Completed	Partially completed	In 2011, agencies published their updated consolidation plans and identified dedicated program managers for their data center consolidation efforts. Also, OMB established a cross-government task force comprised of the agency program managers that meets monthly and launched a public dashboard for tracking progress in closing data centers. However, not all of the agencies' updated data center consolidation plans include the required elements. Of the three agencies we reviewed, one (the Department of Justice) lacked required milestones and targets for servers and utilization. In addition, in February 2012, we reported finding similar gaps in multiple agencies consolidation plans.[a] When asked why the plans were not yet complete, agencies reported that it takes time to adequately plan for data center consolidation and many found that they need more time. We have previously recommended that agencies complete the missing elements from their data center consolidation plans.[b]
(3) Shift to cloud-first policy	Completed	Partially completed	The Federal CIO published a strategy for moving the government to cloud computing and had each agency identify three services to be moved to the cloud. In addition, each of the three agencies we reviewed established migration plans for these services and had migrated at least one service to the cloud by December 2011. However, each of the three agencies' migration plans we reviewed were missing key required elements, including a discussion of needed resources, migration schedules, or plans for retiring legacy systems. We have ongoing work performing a more detailed review of seven agencies' progress in implementing the federal cloud computing policy underway, and plan to issue that report in the summer of 2012.[c]
(4) Stand-up contract vehicles for secure Infrastructure-as-a-Service solutions	Completed	Completed	GSA has established a common set of contract vehicles for secure cloud-based infrastructure solutions, and made them available governmentwide. As of January 2012, federal agencies could purchase cloud solutions from three GSA-approved vendors.

Plan number and action item title	OMB's reported status (as of December 2011)	GAO's assessment	Description
(10) Launch a best practices collaboration platform	Completed	Partially completed	The CIO Council developed a web-based collaboration portal to allow program managers to exchange best practices and case studies, and all three agencies we reviewed have submitted case studies to OMB for the portal. However, the data accessible by the portal has not yet been effectively codified and synthesized, making it difficult for program managers to search the databases and for them to use it for problem solving. For example, a general search for cloud computing best practices identified more than 13,000 artifacts, while a date-bounded search for the last year identified 14 artifacts—of which only 8 clearly provided information on best practices in cloud computing. The vice chairman of the CIO Council explained that the portal's shortcomings are due to how new it is, and noted that the council is still working to improve the portal's functionality.
(13) Design a cadre of specialized IT acquisition professionals	Completed	Completed	In 2011, OFPP issued guidance defining an IT acquisition specialist; established the requirements, guidance, curriculum, and process for becoming one; and established guidance to strengthen the IT acquisition skills and capabilities of IT acquisition specialists. Because the development of the cadre is voluntary, the status of the agencies we reviewed varies: the Department of Veterans Affairs has a cadre of specialized IT acquisition professionals, the Department of Homeland Security is developing one, and the Department of Justice is still considering whether they need such a cadre.
(15) Issue contracting guidance and templates to support modular development	Partially completed	Partially completed	An OFPP official stated that the agency worked with the IT and acquisition community to develop draft guidance for modular development, and has obtained feedback from industry leaders. However, OFPP has not yet issued this guidance, or the required templates and samples supporting modular development. An OFPP official explained that delays were due to challenges in ensuring consistent definitions of modular development across the government and industry.
(17) Work with Congress to create IT budget models that align with modular development	Partially completed	Partially completed	OMB reported that it analyzed existing legal frameworks to determine what budget flexibilities are currently available and where additional budget flexibilities are needed, and worked to promote these ideas (such as multiyear budgets or revolving funds) with selected congressional committees. Also, the three agencies we reviewed identified programs where additional budget flexibilities could improve outcomes. For example, the Department of Homeland Security proposed a working capital fund for centralized IT

Table 2. (Continued)

Plan number and action item title	OMB's reported status (as of December 2011)	GAO's assessment	Description
			operations and maintenance functions. However, in response to OM s, there has not yet been any new legislation to create budget authorities as a result of the IT Reform Plan and OMB has not identified options to increase transparency for programs that would fall under these budgetary flexibilities. OMB officials noted that they are behind schedule in working with Congress, in part because when the IT Reform Plan was issued in December 2010, the fiscal year 2012 budget process was already under way. They explained that this meant they needed to wait to incorporate changes into the fiscal year 2013 budget process.
(20) Work with Congress to consolidate commodity IT spending under agency CIOs	Partially completed	Partially completed	OMB issued a memo in August 2011 that, among other things, required agencies to consolidate commodity IT services under the agency CIO.[d] In addition, the federal CIO has discussed the importance of consolidating commodity IT under the agency CIOs with selected congressional committees. However, OMB noted that this action item is behind schedule and that it is continuing to discuss the implementation of the memo and the development of models for funding commodity IT with agencies and Congress. Further, the three agencies we reviewed had not yet reported to OMB on their proposals for migrating commodity IT services to shared services, in part because they were waiting for guidance from OMB. OMB officials noted that part of the reason for the delay is that when the IT Reform plan was issued in December 2010, the fiscal year 2012 budget process was already under way. Therefore, they needed to wait a year to incorporate changes into the fiscal year 2013 budget process.
(21) Reform and strengthen Investment Review Boards	Completed	Completed	In 2011, OMB revamped its requirements for agency IT budget submissions. OMB also developed, published, and provided training for agency CIOs on how to conduct TechStat reviews that includes accountability guidelines, engagement cadence, evaluation processes, and reporting processes. By December 2011, all 24 agencies conducted at least one TechStat review.
(22) Redefine role of agency CIOs	Completed	Partially completed	In August 2011, OMB issued a memo directing agencies to strengthen the role of the CIO away from solely being responsible for policymaking and infrastructure maintenance to a

Plan number and action item title	OMB's reported status (as of December 2011)	GAO's assessment	Description
and the CIO Council			role that encompasses true portfolio management for all IT. However, OMB acknowledged that there is disparity among agency CIOs' authorities and that it will take time for agencies to implement the required changes. Of the three agencies we reviewed, two CIOs reported having true portfolio management for all IT projects, and one did not. The Department of Homeland Security's CIO does not yet have responsibility for the portfolio of all IT projects. We have ongoing work assessing the Department's governance of IT investments. Regarding changes in the role of the CIO Council, the council formed a committee to focus on management best practices. This committee analyzed the outcomes of agency TechStat reviews over the past year and published a report discussing governmentwide trends in December 2011.

Source: GAO analysis of OMB and agency data.

[a] GAO

[b] GAO

[c] The seven agencies are the Departments of Agriculture, Health and Human Services, Homeland Security, State, and Treasury, as well as the General Services Administration and the Small Business Administration.

[d] OMB, Memorandum for Heads of Executive Departments and Agencies: Chief Information Officer Authorities, M-11-29 (Washington, D.C.: Aug. 8, 2011).

OMB and the agencies have plans for addressing all seven of the action items that we identified as behind schedule, but lack time frames for completing five of them. The seven action items we identified are:

- *Data center consolidation.* We noted that agencies' data center consolidation plans do not include all required elements. In July 2011, OMB directed agencies to complete the missing elements in their plans. The agencies are expected to provide an update on their plans in September 2012.
- *Cloud-first policy.* We noted that agencies' migration plans were missing selected elements. An OMB official stated while OMB did not review the quality of agency migration plans in order to close the reform plan action item, the official responsible for the cloud-first initiative would continue to work with agencies to ensure that the initiative was successful. There are no time frames for agencies to complete their migration plans.
- *Best practice collaboration portal.* We found that the best practices collaboration platform is missing key features that would allow the information to be accessible and useable. A CIO Council official noted that the council plans to improve the portal over time by adding the ability to load artifacts, allow users to chat online, contain an expertise repository, and allow or encourage labeling of information to improve the search for artifacts within the platform. However, the CIO Council has not established a time frame for providing additional functionality to the web-based collaboration portal.
- *Guidance and templates for modular contracting.* OFPP has not issued guidance or the required templates and samples supporting modular development. It plans to continue developing guidance and templates to support modular development, and the first draft of this guidance is currently undergoing initial review. OFPP plans to issue its guidance and templates in spring 2012.
- *Obtaining new IT budget authorities.* OMB is behind schedule in obtaining new IT budget authorities. OMB officials stated that it plans to propose new authorities as part of the 2013 President's Budget, and intends to work with congressional committees throughout the budget rollout process. However, OMB has not yet established time frames for completing this activity.
- *Consolidating commodity IT under the agency CIO.* OMB is behind schedule in consolidating commodity IT spending under agency CIOs.

OMB plans to propose new spending models for commodity IT in the 2013 President's Budget, and to work with Congress to implement these new models. However, OMB has not established a time frame for completing this activity.

- *Redefining roles of agency CIOs and the CIO Council.* OMB acknowledges that not all agency CIOs have authority for a full portfolio of IT investments and plans to collect data from agencies during spring 2012 to determine the extent to which the CIOs have this authority. At that point, OMB should be better positioned to determine what more needs to be done to ensure CIO roles are redefined. However, there is no time frame for completing this activity.

Until OMB and the agencies establish time frames for completing corrective actions, they increase the risk that key actions will not be effectively managed to closure. For example, without cloud migration plans, agencies risk maintaining legacy systems long after the system has been replaced by one operating in the cloud. Further, these incomplete actions reduce the likelihood of achieving the full range of benefits promised by the IT reform initiatives.

OMB HAS NOT ESTABLISHED MEASURES FOR EVALUATING RESULTS ON MOST IT REFORM INITIATIVES

The importance of performance measures for gauging the progress of programs and projects is well recognized. In the past, OMB has directed agencies to define and select meaningful outcome-based performance measures that track the intended results of carrying out a program or activity.[26] Additionally, as we have previously reported, aligning performance measures with goals can help to measure progress toward those goals, emphasizing the quality of the services an agency provides or the resulting benefits to users.[27] Furthermore, industry experts describe performance measures as necessary for managing, planning, and monitoring the performance of a project against plans and stakeholders' needs.[28] According to government and industry best practices, performance measures should be measurable, outcome-oriented, and actively tracked and managed.

Recognizing the importance of performance measurement, OMB and GSA have established measures for 4 of the 10 action items we reviewed: data center consolidation, shifting to cloud computing, using contract vehicles to obtain Infrastructure-as-a-Service, and reforming investment review boards. Moreover, OMB reported on three of these measures in the analytical perspectives associated with the President's fiscal year 2013 budget. Specifically, regarding data center consolidation, OMB reported that agencies were on track to close 525 centers by the end of 2012 and expected to save $3 billion by 2015. On the topic of cloud computing, OMB reported that agencies had migrated 40 services to cloud computing environments in 2011 and expect to migrate an additional 39 services in 2012. Regarding investment review boards, OMB reported that agency CIOs held 294 TechStat reviews and had achieved more than $900 million in cost savings, life cycle cost avoidance, or reallocation of funding.

However, OMB has not established performance measures for 6 of the 10 action items we reviewed. For example, OMB has not established measures related to the best practices collaboration platform, such as number of users, number of hits per query, and customer satisfaction. Further, while OMB has designed the guidance and curriculum for developing a cadre of IT acquisition professionals, it has not established measures for tracking agencies development of such a cadre. Table 3 details what performance measures and goals, if any, are associated with the action item.

OMB officials, including two policy analysts within the Office of E-government and Information Technology who are responsible for the IT Reform Plan, stated that they do not believe that it is appropriate for OMB to establish measures for the action items in the IT Reform Plan. The officials explained that they believe that the purpose of the IT Reform Plan is to act as a catalyst for initiatives that are expected to continue outside of the plan. For example, the IT Reform Plan called for OMB and agencies to complete several discrete activities to push forward on data center consolidation, but the Federal Data Center Consolidation Initiative will continue on well after the deliverables noted in the reform plan are completed. They acknowledged that it would be appropriate to have performance measures for each of the broader initiatives outside of the IT Reform Plan, but noted that this should be the responsibility of the group running each initiative.

We disagree with OMB's view and believe that performance measures are a powerful way to motivate people, communicate priorities, and improve performance.

Table 3. Assessment of Performance Measures Associated with Selected IT Reform Action Items

Action item	Performance measures	Performance goals
(1) Complete detailed implementation plans to consolidate 800 data centers by 2015	• Number of data center closures • Expected cost savings	• The IT Reform Plan identifies a goal to consolidate 800 data centers by 2015. • In December 2011, in conjunction with a decision to include smaller data centers in the consolidation effort, the Federal CIO increased this goal to more than 1000 data centers by 2015. • In February 2012, OMB announced a goal of saving $3 billion by 2015.
(3) Shift to a cloud-first policy	• Number of services transitioned to a cloud computing environment • Number of legacy systems eliminated • Anticipated cost savings	• The IT Reform Plan states that each agency will identify three services to move to the cloud and that one of those services must move within 12 months. • OMB has not yet announced goals for eliminated legacy systems or anticipated cost savings.
(4) Stand-up contract vehicles	• Number of task orders issued under the	• GSA established a goal of having at least one task order issued under
for secure Infrastructure-as-a-Service solutions	contract vehicle • Dollar amounts awarded through the contract vehicle • Period of performance for the contract	Infrastructure-as-a-Service blanket the purchase agreement in the first year. • GSA has not yet announced goals for its second year.
(10) Launch a best practices collaboration platform	—[a]	—[a]
(13) Design a cadre of specialized IT acquisition professionals	—[a]	—[a]
(15) Issue contracting guidance and templates to support modular development	—[a]	—[a]
(17) Work with Congress to create IT budget models that align with modular development	—[a]	—[a]
(20) Work with Congress to consolidate commodity IT spending under agency CIOs	—[a]	—[a]

Table 3. (Continued)

Action item	Performance measures	Performance goals
(21) Reform and strengthen investment review boards	• Number of TechStat reviews • Number of terminated Programs • Cost savings associated with TechStat reviews	• OMB established a goal of having agency CIOs terminate or turn around one third of all underperforming IT investments by June 2012.
(22) Redefine role of agency CIOs and the CIO Council	—[a]	—[a]

Source: GAO analysis of OMB and agency data.
[a] Performance measures or goals have not been established for this action item.

In our assessment, we sought any available performance measures associated with either the action item or the broader initiative, and in cases like the data center consolidation initiative, gave credit for the measures that were established for the initiative. However, we found that most action items and initiatives lacked any performance measures. Moreover, if OMB encourages individual agencies to establish measures, there will likely be multiple different measures for the action items and it would be more difficult to demonstrate governmentwide progress. Therefore, we believe that it is appropriate for OMB to establish performance measures for each of the action items in order to effectively measure the results of the IT Reform Plan. Until OMB establishes and begins tracking measurable, outcome-oriented performance measures for each of the action items, the agency will be limited it its ability to evaluate progress that has been made and whether or not the initiative is achieving its goals.

CONCLUSION

OMB and selected agencies have made strides in implementing the IT Reform Plan, including pushing agencies to consolidate data centers, migrating federal services to cloud computing, improving the skills of IT acquisition professionals, and strengthening the roles and accountability of CIOs. However, several key reform items are behind schedule and OMB lacks time frames for completing most of them. Despite reporting that selected actions are completed, OMB and federal agencies are still working on them. This sends an inconsistent message on the need to maintain focus on these important initiatives. Moving forward, it will be important for OMB to accurately characterize the status of the action items in the IT Reform Plan in order to keep agencies' focus and momentum on these important reform initiatives.

OMB has not established performance measures for gauging the success of most of its reform initiatives. For example, while OMB is tracking the number of services that agencies move to a cloud computing environment and the number of data center closures, it is not tracking the usefulness of its efforts to develop a best practices collaboration portal or a cadre of IT acquisition professionals.

Until OMB and the agencies complete the action items called for in the IT Reform Plan, establish time frames for completing corrective actions, and establish performance measures to track the results of the reform initiatives, the government may not be able to realize the full promise of the IT Reform Plan. The IT Reform Plan's goals of improving government IT acquisitions and the efficiency of government operations are both ambitious and important, and they warrant a more structured approach to ensure actions are completed and results are achieved.

RECOMMENDATIONS FOR EXECUTIVE ACTION

To help ensure the success of IT reform initiatives, we are making four recommendations to OMB. Specifically we are recommending that the Director of the Office of Management and Budget direct the Federal Chief Information Officer to

- ensure that the action items called for in the IT Reform Plan are completed by the responsible parties prior to the completion of the IT Reform Plan's 18 month deadline of June 2012, or if the June 2012 deadline cannot be met, by another clearly defined deadline;
- provide clear time frames for addressing the shortfalls associated with the IT Reform Plan action items;
- accurately characterize the status of the IT Reform Plan action items in the upcoming progress report in order to keep momentum going on action items that are not yet completed; and
- establish outcome-oriented measures for each applicable action item in the IT Reform Plan.

We are also making two recommendations to the Secretaries of Homeland Security and Veterans Affairs and to the Attorney General of the Department of Justice to address action items in the IT Reform Plan where the agencies have fallen behind. Specifically, we are recommending that they direct their respective agency CIOs to

- complete elements missing from the agencies' plans for migrating services to a cloud computing environment, as applicable, and
- identify and report on the commodity services proposed for migration to shared services.

AGENCY COMMENTS AND OUR EVALUATION

We received comments on a draft of our report from OMB; the Departments of Homeland Security, Justice, and Veterans Affairs; and GSA. OMB agreed with two recommendations and disagreed with two recommendations; the Departments of Homeland Security, Justice, and Veterans Affairs generally agreed with our recommendations; and GSA did not agree or disagree with our recommendations. Each agency's comments are discussed in more detail below.

- OMB's Federal CIO provided written comments on a draft of this report, as well as supplementary comments via e-mail. The Federal CIO stated that OMB believes our analysis and findings have been critical to driving IT reforms across the federal government, and that OMB plans to use this report to continue the positive momentum on the IT Reform Plan. In addition, the Federal CIO stated that despite agreeing with many of the observations and recommendations in the draft report, OMB had concerns with selected recommendations, observations, and the scope of our review. The agency's comments and, where applicable, our evaluation follow:
  - OMB agreed with our recommendation to ensure that action items called for in the IT Reform Plan are completed by the end of the IT Reform Plan's 18-month deadline of June 2012 and stated that OMB intends to complete the action items by the deadline.
  - OMB agreed with our recommendation to provide clear time frames for addressing the shortfalls associated with the IT Reform

Plan action items and stated that OMB will provide clear time frames where applicable.

- OMB disagreed with our recommendation that the agency accurately characterize the status of IT Reform Plan action items in the upcoming progress report. The agency stated that it has accurately characterized the completeness of the action items, and therefore, the recommendation does not apply. As stated in this report, we do not agree with OMB's characterization of four action items: data center consolidation, cloud-first policy, best practices collaboration portal, and redefining roles of agency CIOs and the CIO Council. OMB considers these action items to be completed. We do not.

  While OMB has made progress in each of these areas, we found activities specified in the IT Reform Plan that have not yet been completed. Specifically, in the area of data center consolidation, we found that selected agency plans are still incomplete; in the move to cloud computing, selected agency migration plans lack key elements; in the area of the best practices portal, we found that the portal lacks key features that would allow the information to be accessible and useful to program managers; and in revising CIO roles, we identified an agency that does not yet have the envisioned authority over IT acquisitions. Further, in a recent memorandum to agency CIOs, the Federal CIO acknowledged that agency data center consolidation plans are incomplete and required agencies to provide an annual update to the plans.[29] In addition, our assessment that the cloud migration plans are incomplete was affirmed by the three agencies we reviewed agreeing with our recommendation that they complete cloud migration plans. Thus, we believe that our recommendation to OMB to accurately characterize the status of IT Reform action items is valid.

- OMB disagreed with our recommendation to establish outcome-oriented measures for each applicable action item in the IT Reform Plan, noting that the agency measured the completeness of the IT Reform actions and not the performance measures associated with broader initiatives. OMB also suggested that we erroneously gave the agency credit for performance measures associated with broader initiatives on data center consolidation, cloud computing, and investment review boards. We acknowledge that some of the action items in the IT Reform Plan are subsets of broader initiatives, and where applicable, we gave credit for having measures associated with the broader initiatives. We continue to believe that this approach is appropriate because the action items and the broader initiatives are intrinsically intertwined. For instance, it would have been unfair to state that there are no measures associated with consolidating federal data centers when such measures clearly exist.

Moreover, the point remains that there are multiple action items in the IT Reform Plan that are not aligned with broader initiatives and for which there are no measures. Examples include the best practices portal, development of a cadre of specialized IT acquisition professionals, and establishing budget models that align with modular development. Given that the purpose of the IT Reform Plan is to achieve operational efficiencies and improve the management of large-scale IT programs, we continue to assert that it is appropriate to establish performance measures to monitor the IT Reform Plan's results. According to the administration's public website intended to provide a window on efforts to deliver a more effective, smarter, and leaner government, performance measurement is a necessary step in improving performance and that it helps set priorities, tailor actions, inform on progress, and diagnose problems.[30] Until OMB establishes and tracks measureable, outcome-oriented performance measures for each of the action items in the IT Reform Plan, the agency will be limited in its ability to evaluate progress that has been made and whether or not the initiative is achieving its goals.

- OMB stated that the title of our draft report (*Information Technology Reform: Progress is Mixed; More Needs to Be Done to Complete Actions and Measure Results*) did not accurately capture the substantial and overwhelmingly positive progress made to date. Moreover, OMB stated that the responsible entities have completed 81.5 percent of the required activities associated with the 10 action items we reviewed. We acknowledge the progress OMB and agencies have made on IT Reform Plan items in this report and have modified the title of our report to reflect that progress. However, our analysis of the percentage of completed activities differs from OMB's calculations. The 10 action items we reviewed include 31 distinct required activities (see table 1). We found that the responsible entities completed 18 of these activities—a 58 percent completion rate.

- OMB also stated that our assessment should acknowledge that OMB does not have the statutory authority to carry out certain action items without congressional action. These action items involved creating IT budget models to align with modular development and consolidating commodity IT spending under the agency CIOs. The Federal CIO stated that although OMB has taken steps to engage with Congress, the agency cannot unilaterally grant budget flexibilities or consolidate spending. While it is true that completing these items depends upon congressional action, according to the IT Reform Plan, it is the responsibility of OMB and the federal agencies to work with Congress to propose budget models to address these items.

- In general, OMB stated that it will continue to drive reform throughout the federal government via the completion of the remaining actions in the IT Reform Plan, as well as continuing to work with agencies as they implement broader initiatives such as data center consolidation and the transition to cloud computing.

- In supplementary comments provided via e-mail, the Federal CIO also expressed concerns with the scope of our report, stating that the intent of the IT Reform Plan was not to reform all federal IT, but to establish some early wins to garner momentum for OMB's broader initiatives. The Federal CIO also noted that OMB has been consistent in publicizing the IT Reform Plan as an 18-month plan with discrete goals designed to augment and accelerate broader initiatives that existed before the IT Reform Plan was launched and would continue after the plan has been completed.

We believe that the scope of our review is appropriate. Since its inception, the scope of our review has focused on the action items and supporting activities noted in the IT Reform Plan. All of the required activities listed in table 1 in the background section of this report are listed in the IT Reform Plan. Moreover, we did not evaluate activities that are outside of the IT Reform Plan, such as OMB's efforts to establish a cost model for agencies to use in estimating the costs and savings of data center consolidation. Further, we agree that to completely reform IT, OMB and agencies must undertake activities beyond the IT Reform Plan's 18-month time frame. The activities within the IT Reform Plan are essential building blocks that will carry on well beyond the IT Reform Plan's end.

- In written comments, the Department of Homeland Security's Director of Departmental GAO-Office of Inspector General Liaison Office concurred with our recommendations and identified steps that the agency is undertaking to address them.
- In written comments, the Department of Justice's Assistant Attorney General for Administration generally agreed with our recommendations and identified steps that the agency has undertaken to address them.
- In written comments, the Chief of Staff at the Department of Veterans Affairs agreed with our recommendations and identified steps that the department is taking to implement them.
- In comments provided via e-mail, a Management and Program Analyst within GSA's Office of Administrative Services stated that the agency had no official response or technical comments on the draft report.

David A. Powner
Director, Information Technology Management Issues

APPENDIX I. OBJECTIVES, SCOPE, AND METHODOLOGY

Our objectives were to (1) evaluate the progress the Office of Management and Budget (OMB) and key federal agencies have made on selected action items in the Information Technology (IT) Reform Plan, (2) assess the plans for addressing any action items that are behind schedule, and (3) assess the extent to which sound measures are in place to evaluate the success of the IT reform initiatives.

In establishing the scope of our engagement, we selected ten action items for review, focusing on action items that (1) were due at the 6 or 12 month milestones because these were expected to be completed during our review, (2) covered multiple different topic areas, and (3) were considered by internal and OMB subject matter experts to be the more important items. These action items are:

- Complete detailed implementation plans to consolidate 800 data centers by 2015.

- Shift to a "cloud first" policy.
- Stand-up contract vehicles for secure Infrastructure-as-a-Service solutions.
- Launch a best practices collaboration platform.
- Design a cadre of specialized IT acquisition professionals.
- Issue contracting guidance and templates to support modular development.
- Work with Congress to create IT budget models that align with modular development.
- Work with Congress to consolidate Commodity IT spending under agency Chief Information Officers (CIO).
- Reform and strengthen Investment Review Boards.
- Redefine the role of agency CIOs and the CIO Council.

In addition, in the seven cases where multiple agencies are identified as a responsible entity for the action item, we selected three civilian agencies (the Departments of Homeland Security, Veterans Affairs, and Justice) based on factors including (1) high levels of IT spending in fiscal year 2011, (2) poor performance on the IT Dashboard, (3) high number of major IT investments in fiscal year 2011, and (4) coverage of agencies that were not included on other GAO reviews of IT reform initiatives.

To evaluate OMB and federal agencies progress in implementing the IT Reform Plan, we evaluated efforts by the entities responsible for each of the action items, including OMB, the General Services Administration (GSA), the Chief Information Officers (CIO) Council, and selected agencies. For each of the 10 action items in the IT Reform Plan, we reviewed OMB's guidance and identified required activities. We compared agency documentation to these requirements, and identified gaps and missing elements. We rated each action item as "completed" if the responsible agencies demonstrated that they completed the required activities on or near the due date, and "partially completed" if the agencies demonstrated that they completed part of the required activities. We interviewed agency officials to clarify our initial findings and to determine why elements were incomplete or missing.

To assess the plans for addressing any action items that are behind schedule, we identified the agencies' plans for addressing the schedule shortfalls and compared these to sound project planning practices identified by organizations recognized for their experience in project management and acquisition processes.[31] We also interviewed relevant agency officials regarding the reasons that their activities were behind schedule and the impact of any shortfalls in their mitigation plans.

To assess the extent to which sound measures are in place to evaluate success, we determined whether performance measures were applicable for each of the selected action items, and if so, how agencies were tracking these measures. We compared these measures to best practices in IT performance management identified by leading industry and government organizations [32] and assessed other options for measuring performance. In addition, we interviewed OMB and selected agency officials regarding progress, plans, and measures. As we were completing our audit work, OMB reported making progress in its efforts to consolidate data centers, transition to a cloud computing environment, and strengthen investment review boards, and provided data on specific measures within each of these areas. We assessed the reliability of the data provided on these measures by obtaining information from agency officials and from the CIO Council regarding their efforts to ensure the reliability of the data. While we identified limitations in the quality of the data that agencies reported, we determined that this data was sufficiently reliable for the purpose of presenting a general overview of progress in establishing performance measures.

We conducted our work at multiple agencies' headquarters in the Washington, D.C., metropolitan area. We conducted this performance audit from August 2011 to April 2012 in accordance with generally accepted government auditing standards. Those standards require that we plan and perform the audit to obtain sufficient, appropriate evidence to provide a reasonable basis for our findings and conclusions based on our audit objectives. We believe that the evidence obtained provides a reasonable basis for our findings and conclusions based on our audit objectives.

End Notes

[1] The Federal Chief Information Officer is a position within the Office of Management and Budget.

[2] See Carnegie Mellon University's are Engineering Institute, *Capability Maturity Model® Integration for Acquisition, Version 1.3* (CMMI-ACQ, V1.3) and Project Management Institute Inc., *A Guide to the Project Management Body of Knowledge (PMBOK® Guide)– Fourth Edition*, (Newtown Square, PA: 2008).

[3] See OMB, *Guide to the Program Assessment Rating Tool* (Washington, D.C.: January 2008); Department of the Navy, Office of the Chief Information Officer, *Guide for Developing and Using Information Technology (IT) Performance Measurements* (Washington, D.C.: October 2001); and General Services Administration, Office of Governmentwide Policy,

Performance-Based Management: Eight Steps To Develop and Use Information Technology Performance Measures Effectively (Washington, D.C.: 1996).

[4] 44 U.S.C. § 3501 et seq.

[5] 40 U.S.C. § 11101 et seq.

[6] The E-Government Act of 2002, Pub. L. No. 107-347 (Dec. 17, 2002).

[7] Pub. L. No. 111-352, 124 Stat. 3866 (2011). The GPRA (Government Performance and Results Act) Modernization Act of 2010 amends the Government Performance and Results Act of 1993, Pub. L. No. 103-62, 107 Stat. 285 (1993).

[8] 31 U.S.C. § 1120(a)(1)(B).

[9] OMB, *25 Point Implementation Plan to Reform Federal Information Technology Management,* (Washington, D.C.: Dec. 9, 2010).

[10] GAO, *Data Center Consolidation: Agencies Need to Complete Inventories and Plans to Achieve Expected Savings,* GAO-11-565 (Washington, D.C.: July 19, 2011).

[11] GAO, *Follow-up on 2011 Report: Status of Actions Taken to Reduce Duplication, Overlap, and Fragmentation, Save Tax Dollars, and Enhance Revenue,* GAO-12-453SP (Washington, D.C.: Feb. 28, 2012).

[12] GAO, *Information Security: Federal Guidance Needed to Address Control Issues with Implementing Cloud Computing,* GAO-10-513 (Washington, D.C.: May 27, 2010).

[13] GAO, *Information Security: Additional Guidance Needed to Address Cloud Computing Concerns,* GAO-12-130T (Washington, D.C.: Oct. 5, 2011).

[14] GAO, *Information Technology: Critical Factors Underlying Successful Major Acquisitions,* GAO-12-7 (Washington, D.C.: Oct. 21, 2011).

[15] The seven IT investments were identified by department officials as successful acquisitions in that they best achieved their respective cost, schedule, scope, and performance goals.

[16] GAO, *Information Technology: VA Has Taken Important Steps to Centralize Control of Its Resources, but Effectiveness Depends on Additional Planned Actions,* GAO-08-449T (Washington, D.C.: Feb. 13, 2008).

[17] GAO, *Information Technology: Management and Oversight of Projects Totaling Billions of Dollars Need Attention,* GAO-09-624T (Washington, D.C.: Apr. 28, 2009).

[18] GAO, *Information Technology: OMB Can Make More Effective Use of Its Investment Reviews,* GAO-05-276 (Washington, D.C.: Apr. 15, 2005).

[19] GAO, *Information Technology: Agencies and OMB Should Strengthen Processes for Identifying and Overseeing High Risk Projects,* GAO-06-647 (Washington, D.C.: June 15, 2006).

[20] Two different budget submissions, called exhibit 53s and exhibit 300s, provide the data accessible through the IT Dashboard. Exhibit 53s list all of the IT investments and their associated costs within a federal organization. An Exhibit 300, also called the Capital Asset Plan and Business Case, is used to justify resource requests for major IT investments and is intended to enable an agency to demonstrate, to its own management and to OMB, that a major investment is well planned.

[21] GAO, *IT Dashboard: Accuracy Has Improved, and Additional Efforts Are Under Way To Better Inform Decision Making,* GAO-12-210 (Washington, D.C.: Nov. 7, 2011); *Information Technology: OMB Has Made Improvements to Its Dashboard, but Further Work Is Needed by Agencies and OMB to Ensure Data Accuracy,* GAO-11-262 (Washington, D.C.: Mar. 15, 2011); and *Information Technology: OMB's Dashboard Has Increased Transparency and Oversight, but Improvements Needed,* GAO-10-701 (Washington, D.C.: July 16, 2010).

[22] GAO, *Information Technology: OMB Needs to Improve Its Guidance on IT Investments,* GAO-11-826 (Washington, D.C.: Sept. 29, 2011).

[23] GAO, *Federal Chief Information Officers: Opportunities Exist to Improve Role in Information Technology Management,* GAO-11-634 (Washington, D.C.: Sept. 15, 2011).

[24] OMB, *Memorandum for Heads of Executive Departments and Agencies,* M-11-29 (Washington, D.C.: Aug. 8, 2011).

[25] See Carnegie Mellon University's Software Engineering Institute, *Capability Maturity Model® Integration for Acquisition, Version 1.3 (CMMI-ACQ, V1.3)* and Project Management Institute Inc., *A Guide to the Project Management Body of Knowledge (PMBOK® Guide) – Fourth Edition*, (Newtown Square, PA: 2008).

[26] OMB, *Guide to the Program Assessment Rating Tool*.

[27] GAO, *NextGen Air Transportation System: FAA's Metrics Can Be Used to Report on Status of Individual Programs, but Not of Overall NextGen Implementation or Outcomes*, GAO-10-629 (Washington, D.C.: July 27, 2010).

[28] Thomas Wettstein and Peter Kueng, *"A Maturity Model for Performance Measurement Systems,"* and Karen J. Richter, Ph.D., Institute for Defense Analyses, *CMMI® for Acquisition (CMMI-ACQ) Primer, Version 1.2*.

[29] OMB, *Memorandum for Chief Information Officers*, (Washington, D.C.: Mar. 19, 2012).

[30] See www.performance.gov.

[31] See Carnegie Mellon University's Software Engineering Institute, *Capability Maturity Model® Integration for Acquisition, Version 1.3 (CMMI-ACQ, V1.3)* and Project Management Institute Inc., *A Guide to the Project Management Body of Knowledge (PMBOK® Guide)– Fourth Edition*, (Newtown Square, PA: 2008).

[32] See OMB, *Guide to the Program Assessment Rating Tool*; Department of the Navy, *Guide for Developing and Using Information Technology (IT) Performance Measurements*; and General Services Administration, Office of Governmentwide Policy, *Performance-Based Management: Eight Steps To Develop and Use Information Technology Performance Measures Effectively*.

INDEX

D

E

F

G

H

I

L

M

N

O